Including Lower-achievers in the Literacy Hour

Using stories and poems

Collette Drifte

HOPSCOTCH
EDUCATIONAL PUBLISHING

Contents

Chapter 1: Stories and action   6

Chapter 2: Stories and description   14

Chapter 3: Stories and story openings   21

Chapter 4: Poems by significant poets   28

Chapter 5: Poems with word play   36

Chapter 6: Stories with myths and legends   44

Chapter 7: Stories with fables   51

Chapter 8: Traditional stories   58

Chapter 9: Narrative poems   65

Chapter 10: Poems to aid poetry writing   72

Chapter 11: Stories from other cultures   81

Chapter 12: Stories from a point of view   88

Chapter 13: Older stories   95

Chapter 14: Poems from other cultures   102

Chapter 15: Classic poems   110

Generic sheets   118

Published by
Hopscotch Educational Publishing Ltd,
29 Waterloo Place,
Leamington Spa CV32 5LA
Tel: 01926 744227

© 2001 Hopscotch Educational Publishing

Written by Collette Drifte
Series design by Blade Communications
Illustrated by Cathy Gilligan
Printed by Clintplan, Southam

ISBN 1 902239 65 2

About the series

Including Lower-achievers in the Literacy Hour is a series of books aimed at enabling all children, regardless of ability, to access the learning requirements set out in the *National Literacy Strategy Framework for Teaching*. There are six books in the series, one for each of the Primary Years 1–6 (Scottish Primary 2-7). They are designed to be used by teachers or other adults working with lower-achievers in the mainstream classroom.

The books offer a structured approach which provides detailed lesson plans to teach specific skills and goals as outlined in the *National Literacy Strategy Framework for Teaching*. The lesson plans cover work at text, sentence and word levels and target a learning objective from each term's work.

Since lower-achievers often learn at a slower rate than other children, and therefore would have some difficulty in covering the whole year's work within that time, the areas and skills which cause the most problems for these children have been addressed. For example, concepts such as sequencing or predicting are included.

A feature of the series is the provision of several resource and generic sheets for each lesson, which are aimed at considerably reducing teacher preparation time. Permission is granted by the author and publisher to photocopy these sheets for educational purposes within the school or organisation that has purchased this book. The sheets are designed to reinforce the teaching point and offer the child an opportunity to practise the skill being taught. The lesson plans also offer several activities to further consolidate the point. These are designed to be done either with an adult providing close support or with a degree of independence.

The generic sheets can be used with the lesson plans as explained or used by the teacher in a different way according to the needs of the children.

On page 5 is a list of assessment focuses which can be used as an individual assessment record for the children. This page is also photocopiable.

About this book

This book is for teachers of children in Year 5 (Scottish Primary 6). It aims to:

- enable lower-achievers to be introduced to and enjoy a wide range of stories and poems;
- focus on concepts that are essential for the wider development of the literacy skills of lower-achievers;
- encourage lower-achievers to tackle challenging and diverse tasks;
- enable lower-achievers to access aspects of the *National Literacy Strategy Framework for Teaching*.

The book should be seen, however, as part of a wider strategy by the teacher to address the difficulties of lower-achievers. Such children need a great deal of repetition, practice and consolidation. Therefore, the teacher needs to utilise as many resources as possible to ensure a varied approach which offers these.

The professional audience using this book covers a vast range, from the newly qualified teacher (NQT) facing their first class, to the 'old hands' who have many years' experience behind them and from the teacher who has never worked with lower-achievers before, to the classroom assistant who has worked with such children for a long time. Therefore, any scripting or suggestions regarding the delivery of a teaching point can be easily adapted (or even disregarded!) to suit the individual needs of the professional and/or children in question. The whole essence of teaching lower-achievers is to offer individualism and flexibility.

Chapter content

There are three suggested lesson plans in the 'story' chapters and two in the 'poetry' chapters.

Overall aims

These outline the aims for the lessons set out in each chapter.

Featured book/poems

For stories, this section names the book being used, the author and a brief synopsis of the story.

In the case of a poetry chapter, it lists the poems being used, the poet and the page number where there is a photocopiable version of the poems. This can be enlarged for shared reading in the whole-class session.

A feature of all the lesson plans is that the teaching points can be repeated using other texts or poems of the teacher's choice. This is useful if the chosen text is not favoured by the teacher, or if they need to provide more repetition and consolidation of a teaching point.

Intended learning

This sets out the specific aims for each individual lesson within the chapter.

With the whole class

This outlines a whole-class introduction to the lesson. Because the class is together at this point, the lower-achievers will have the support of their peers and also the opportunity to follow the answers to any questions raised by the other children.

With the lower-achievers

This is the main body of the lesson, since it is designed to be done with the lower-achieving group. The adult-led activities are designed to be done together with an adult closely supporting. The activities are designed to utilise an adult, not necessarily the teacher. The independent activities are designed for the lower-achievers to do without as much close support and supervision. However, the term 'independent' does not imply that the child should be left totally unaided or unsupervised. This is something to be decided at the discretion of the adult/teacher, who will know how much the child is capable of doing without support. A lower-achiever may need help at any point in a lesson and should always have access to an adult to provide that help and support.

The activities suggested may be adjusted to suit the needs of the children. They are intended to offer a variety of ways of tackling the same teaching point and are not necessarily a list to be worked through. To cover all the problems of the children would be impossible, so professional judgement has to be used. For example, occasionally cutting and sticking is required, which may be difficult for the child who has problems with motor control – here the adult can assist; some of the activities require writing, so judgement must be used whether the child needs a scribe.

Plenary session

This offers suggestions for what to do with the whole class at the end of the lesson in order to summarise and explore the learning undertaken in the lesson. This should not just be a 'show and tell' session but rather an opportunity for the children to demonstrate their learning. The lower-achievers should be encouraged to play a part in the session.

Acknowledgements

Stories

Why the Whales Came by Michael Morpurgo, (Mammoth, 1985 [1998 edition]); *The Wizard of Oz* by L Frank Baum, (no specific edition recommended); *The Farthest-Away Mountain* by Lynne Reid Banks, (Collins 1988); *The Headless Ghost* by Pete Johnson, (A & C Black 1998); *The Orchard Book of Greek Myths* by Geraldine McCaughrean, (Orchard Books, a division of Watts Publishing Group 1992); *Aesop's Fables* compiled by Russell Ash and Bernard Higton, (Pavilion Books 1990); *Grimms Fairy Tales* translated by Peter Carter, (Oxford University Press, 1997); *The Chilli Challenge and other stories* by Narinder Dhami, Angela Barry and Judith O'Neill, (Heinemann 1998); *War Horse* by Michael Morpurgo, (Collins Educational, 1999); *The Lion, the Witch and the Wardrobe* by C S Lewis, (no specific edition recommended).

Poems

'When we go over to my grandad's' and 'Who Started It?' by Michael Rosen, from *The Puffin Book of Utterly Brilliant Poetry*, edited by Brian Patten, Puffin Books, 1998.

'Going Through the Old Photos' by Michael Rosen, from *A First Poetry Book*, compiled by John Foster, Oxford University Press, 1979 (edition published 1989).

'On and on ...' and 'Gruesome' by Roger McGough, from *The Puffin Book of Utterly Brilliant Poetry*, edited by Brian Patten, Puffin Books, 1998.

'Greedyguts' by Kit Wright, from *The Puffin Book of Utterly Brilliant Poetry*, edited by Brian Patten, Puffin Books, 1998.

'From a Railway Carriage' and 'At the Seaside' by Robert Louis Stevenson, from *A Child's Garden of Verses*, first published 1885.

'Sweet Song' by Vernon Scannell, from *A First Poetry Book* compiled by John Foster, Oxford University Press, 1979 (Edition published 1989), reproduced by permission of the author.

'The Quarrel' by Eleanor Farjeon, from *A First Poetry Book*, compiled by John Foster, Oxford University Press, 1979 (edition published 1989).

'The Pow-Wow Drum' by David Campbell, from *A Caribbean Dozen*, edited by John Agard and Grace Nichols, Walker Books, 1994.

'Sioux Rite of the Sacred Pipe', traditional.

'Windy Nights' by Robert Louis Stevenson, from *A First Poetry Book*, compiled by John Foster, Oxford University Press, 1979 (edition published 1989).

'Echo' by Walter de la Mare, from *Georgian Poets*, selected by James Reeves, Penguin 1968.

List of assessment focuses

Assessment focus	Chapter	Date achieved/comments
Can the child explore the action in texts through pace and delivery, understand how tension in the story is created, understand the difference between direct and reported speech and demonstrate the spelling rule that changes 'y' to 'ies'?	1	
Can the child recognise how description is used to effect in stories, identify and classify 1st, 2nd and 3rd persons in a text and understand and use synonyms?		
Can the child compare different story openings, understand verb tenses and correctly use the spelling rule that changes 'f' to 'ves'?	3	
Can the child appreciate poems by the same poet and recognise the distinct content and style of the poet's work?	4	
Can the child recognise poems which have a play on words, identify how a play on words relates to the meaning of the poem and write own poems to feature a play on words?	5	
Can the child understand and use the terms 'myth' and 'legend', identify the common features of myths and legends, make nouns and verbs agree and distinguish between homophones?	6	
Can the child identify and name the features of a fable, recognise the relationship between nouns and pronouns and recognise and use antonyms?	7	
Can the child recognise and name the common features of traditional stories, identify the ambiguities that can arise from contracted sentences and recognise and use onomatopoeia?	8	
Can the child understand and correctly use the term 'narrative', appreciate narrative poems and write own narrative poem?	9	
Can the child understand rhyming patterns in terms of a,b,c, explore the structure of a poem, and add or substitute own verses to an existing poem?	10	
Can the child appreciate stories from other cultures, understand and use prepositions correctly and recognise how a word is made to mean its opposite by the addition of a prefix?	11	
Can the child appreciate stories written from an unusual point of view, understand and use correctly the apostrophe for possession and transform words to make comparatives?	12	
Can the child appreciate older literature, construct longer sentences using conjunctions and efficiently use dictionaries for abbreviations as well as words?		
Can the child appreciate poems from other cultures and use them as a stimulus to write own poetry?	14	
Can the child read classic poems, explore the language, narrative and poem's time, express personal opinions about the poetry and use poems as a stimulus to explore other classic poetry?	15	

Stories and action

Overall aims

- To explore the action in the text through pace and delivery.
- To understand how tension in the story is created.
- To understand the difference between direct and reported speech.
- To investigate the spelling rule that changes 'y' to 'ies'.

Featured book

Why the Whales Came by Michael Morpurgo, Mammoth, 1985 (1998 edition)

Story synopsis

Gracie and her friend Daniel are warned by everyone to stay away from the mad and dangerous Birdman. But they find that he is a kind and gentle man and they become friends. He tells them to keep off Samson Island because it is cursed, but one foggy night they are forced to land there. When Gracie returns home to find that her father has been killed in the war, she believes in the curse of the island. Only when the friends and the Birdman manage to persuade the other islanders to help rescue a stranded whale can the curse be lifted. Battling against the odds, they send the whale back to the sea and the dark happenings are reversed.

Lesson One

Intended learning

- To explore the action in the text through pace and delivery.
- To understand how tension in the story is created.

With the whole class

Work on the first chapter will take one session. To complete the whole book may take several sessions.

- Ask for a volunteer to read the title of the book and then discuss the illustration on the cover.

What might the book be about? Why is the old man holding up his hand? Challenge the children to suggest why the crowd is armed with sticks and scythes. Why do the children look distressed as they handle the whale? List key words from their suggestions to refer back to at the end of the book.

- Read the first chapter of *Why the Whales Came*. Discuss with the children how the narrative sets the scene and introduces the characters. For example, how do the hints about the mysterious Birdman and the curse of Samson Island help to create atmosphere? Do the children want to find out what happens next? Why? (Remind them of the work they did on chapter endings and cliffhangers in Year 4.)

- Ask the children for suggestions for strategies authors might use to make the reader excited or frightened. Some of the following ideas could be explored:

  – the use of powerful and graphic vocabulary to evoke certain images and create atmosphere and tension (for example, 'Some said the Birdman was mad. Some said he was the devil…', page 14, or 'My mouth was dry with fear…', page 17);
  – the dialogue's pace, delivery and speed (for example, '…the Birdman's only got to touch you and you'll catch it,' page 15);
  – the use of short 'quick' words to convey a faster pace, moving the narrative forward by relating a string of events before slowing up the pace a little.

- Discuss with the children what 'pace' and 'action' mean. Write a few key words on a large sheet of paper to jog memories later.

- Choose a story to retell together in a way that creates tension and atmosphere. For example, 'Jack and the Beanstalk' might be told as, 'Jack was ambling lazily to the market leading the reluctant cow, when suddenly, almost as if out of nowhere, appeared a strange looking old man, who had a frightening glimmer in his eyes and a menacing smile on his face.'

- Now tell the story in a way that creates no tension and is boring. 'Jack was walking to market with his cow when he met an old man.' Can the children see the difference that the use of the language in the first example makes?

■ Explain to the children that they are going to work in groups on activities related to the first chapter of *Why the Whales Came* before reading the rest of the book.

With the lower-achievers

With adult support

Choose from:

1 Explore again the strategies used by the author: the vocabulary (powerful and graphic words), the dialogue, atmosphere and tension, an increase in pace, speeded up action and so on. Make sure the children know what 'pace' and 'action' mean. Together explore Chapter One again for examples and discuss how these are good examples of the strategies. List some of the words the author used for these strategies. Together, think of other sentences to use them in. Do they have the same effect?

2 Give out copies of Resource sheet 1a. Help the children to select and tick the strategies an author might use to create excitement in a story. Give reading help where necessary.

3 Explore other texts for pace, atmosphere and tension. Encourage the children to refer to the strategies written on the large sheet of paper during the whole-class session. They should write a few sentences about what they find.

Teacher-independent activities

Choose from:

1 Give the children copies of Resource sheet 1a to complete, working in pairs for support.

2 Ask the children, working in pairs or groups of three, to choose a fairytale or traditional tale and work together to tell the story, showing the action and creating tension. (Remind them of the story of 'Jack and the Beanstalk' that they worked on during the whole-class session.) They could record their story onto a cassette.

3 Give the children copies of Generic sheet 1 (page 118). Challenge them to tell the story shown in the pictures, first as an exciting story and then to retell it using dull and uninspiring words so that it is not at all exciting. For example, 'One day a fairy cast a spell on the baby. She fell asleep for a hundred years. The prince came and saved her.' It still tells the story but not in an exciting way. They should record their stories onto a cassette.

Plenary session

Before the session, cover up the sheet of paper with the key words that were written in the whole-class session.

■ Invite the children who explored other texts to share with the class what they found. Ask them to read out their work or play their recorded cassettes.

■ Challenge the children to tell you the strategies an author might use to convey the action, set the pace and create tension in a story. Uncover the list and see whether they left any out.

Working with the whole book

■ Over time, read the rest of the book, pausing at appropriate places to explore the tension, action and pace of the story. Explore these passages: page 41, the storm; page 88, dawn on Samson Island; pages 118–19, the struggle to float the whale; pages 126–27, the confrontation between the islanders, and the Birdman, Gracie and Daniel. Ask the children how and why they think these passages create tension. Discuss the language and the vocabulary, the dialogue, the speed of events, the build-up of tension and the creation of atmosphere. Explain again that the choice of words and the pace of the writing are used to help create an atmosphere of urgency.

■ Help the children to role-play one of the episodes, using some of the original dialogue and encouraging them to speak their 'lines' in a way that expresses the action and pace.

Lesson Two

Intended learning

- To understand the difference between direct and reported speech.

- To use the text as a basis for exploring examples of direct and reported speech.

With the whole class

- Ask several of the children a simple question such as *"Lucy, why do you have to eat?"* or *"Pritpal, what did you do this morning?"* When they have answered, write their answers on the board. *"So that I can stay alive"* or *'Maths, and then I went swimming'*. Remember to put in the speech marks (either double or single).

- Ask the children why there are speech marks punctuating the answers. Tell them that this is called 'direct speech' because it refers to the words that come directly from the person speaking. Write 'direct speech' on the board above the examples.

- Tell the children to listen carefully to what you are going to say next. Write on the board an example of reported speech from the children's answers, such as 'Lucy said that she has to eat so that she can stay alive.' Write this without inverted commas. Ask for volunteers to tell you the difference between the examples. They should mention that there aren't any speech marks, that you used the phrase 'Lucy said', that the pronouns changed and the verbs changed to agree, that the original question is included in the sentence and that you used the word 'that' before reporting what Lucy said. Explain that this is called reported speech because somebody is telling (or reporting) what another person has said. Ask for volunteers to change the other examples into reported speech. Write 'reported speech' on the board above them.

- Play a game where Child A makes a statement such as 'I had porridge for breakfast,' to Child B. Child B states it as reported speech – 'He said he had porridge for breakfast.' Then Child B makes a statement for Child C, and so on.

- Explore the chosen text for some examples of direct speech. Ask the children to tell you how these would be written as reported speech. Then look at some examples of reported speech (pages 15, 49, 87 and 135) and ask the children how these would be written as direct speech. Encourage the children to suggest reasons why reported speech is used in writing. For example, we as readers can learn what another character's opinion is, what they have said in an 'off-stage' situation or a piece of information relevant to the story that otherwise we wouldn't have known; the author can tell us these pieces of information without having to write another (possibly irrelevant) scene.

- Remind the children that we often see direct speech in the form of speech bubbles. Choose one of the pieces of direct speech that the children used in their game, such as 'I had porridge for breakfast' and write it on the board inside a speech bubble.

With the lower-achievers

With adult support

Choose from:

1   Make sure the children fully understand both direct and reported speech. If necessary, explore the text for a few more examples in order to consolidate the point. Ask them to convert direct to reported speech and vice versa. Look at a few stories together and change the examples of direct speech to reported speech. For example, 'Mr Twit told Mrs Twit that she had the worst case of the shrinks that he had ever seen,' or 'Lucy told Peter that she went into the wardrobe just after breakfast and that she'd been away for hours and hours.' Help the children to write these, sometimes using speech bubbles for the direct speech.

2   Remind the children that we sometimes use speech bubbles to show direct speech and then give them copies of Resource sheet 1b and help them to write the examples of direct and reported speech in their opposite forms. Give reading help if necessary.

3   Prepare a set of cards, half with examples of direct speech and half with reported speech. Play a game together where the cards are mixed

up and placed face down on the table. The children take a card, read it aloud, say what kind of speech it is and then tell you the opposite form. If they are correct, they take a token. The winner is the child with the highest number of tokens at the end of the game.

Teacher-independent activities

Choose from:

1   Give the children copies of Resource sheet 1b to complete. Remind them that speech bubbles are sometimes used to show direct speech.

2   Prepare a set of cards, half with examples of direct speech and half with reported speech. Ask the children to work in pairs to decide the opposite form of each card. They should write the examples of reported speech and record onto a cassette the examples of direct speech. If independent writing is too difficult, they could record all the examples.

3   Ask the children to work in pairs and give each pair an old comic. Ask them to cut out examples of speech bubbles and stick them onto a sheet of paper. They should then write beside each one the reported speech form. For example, they could stick a picture of Dennis the Menace saying, 'Get lost, Sherbert Sucker!' and then write, 'Dennis told Sherbert Sucker to get lost.'

Plenary session

■   Ask for volunteers to tell the class what reported and direct speech are. What are the advantages of reported speech?

■   Ask the children who completed resource sheets or played games to explain to the others what they had to do. If anybody made cassette recordings, let them play them to the class.

■   Does everybody understand the differences between direct and reported speech? What did the children find particularly difficult about the lesson?

Lesson Three

Intended learning

■   To investigate the spelling rule that changes 'y' to 'ies'.

■   To use the text as a basis for exploring examples of this rule.

■   To practise applying the rule.

With the whole class

■   Write on the board a collection of nouns that end in 'y', for example, 'baby', 'story', 'body' and 'jelly'. Ask the children if they think these are singular or plural. If necessary, spend a few moments exploring and revising singulars and plurals. Tell the children that to write these words in the plural, they need to change the spelling. Does anybody know what to do? Challenge them to come to the board and point out how each word needs to change.

■   Draw a clear line between the body of the word and the final 'y'. Cross out the 'y' and write 'ies' beside it in a different colour. Encourage volunteers to come to the board and rewrite the complete new words.

■   Ask the children to give you examples of nouns that end in 'ies', for example 'ladies', 'families', 'spies' and 'countries'. Invite them to write them on the board. Are these singular or plural? What are the singulars of these words? How do we spell them? Draw a clear line between the body of the word and the final 'ies'. Cross out the 'ies' and write 'y' beside it in a different colour. Encourage volunteers to come to the board and rewrite the complete new words.

■   Explain to the children that all singular words that end in 'consonant + y' change to 'consonant + ies' in the plural.

■   Warn the children that for words that have a vowel before the 'y' they just add an 's' for the plural, for example 'valley', 'valleys'; 'tray', 'trays'; 'convoy', 'convoys' and 'buy', 'buys'. Tell them to be on the lookout for other words that might have a slightly different rule and discuss them as they arise throughout the lesson.

■ Read to them from *Why the Whales Came* for examples of words with this spelling rule: page 21 'stories', page 57 'authorities', page 66 'armies' and page 105 'spies'. Ask for volunteers to come to the board and write these in the singular.

With the lower-achievers

With adult support

Choose from:

1 Prepare two sets of cards, one of 'consonant + y' words and the other of 'ies' words. Use easy words such as those used in the whole-class session. Choose a question-master/mistress. This person takes a card from one of the two piles and holds it up for the others to read. The others race to write down the plural or singular version of the word, using whiteboards. The first person to hold up the correct answer becomes the new question-master/mistress.

2 Give out copies of Resource sheet 1c. Work closely with them to complete it.

3 Give the children copies of Generic sheet 2 (page 119) with some consonant + 'y' words and some 'ies' words. Help them to learn to spell the words using the 'Look, Say, Cover, Write, Check' strategy.

Teacher-independent activities

Choose from:

1 Prepare a recorded cassette with both singular and plural words ('y' and 'ies'). Make sure you leave enough time between each word to allow for switching the recorder off and on. You could also give the children a card with the words listed in order of recording. They should listen to the word and then write its other form. Challenge them to record sentences for two or three of each type.

2 Give the children copies of Resource sheet 1c to complete.

3 Have prepared a set of cards half with 'consonant + y' words and half with 'ies' words written on them and each with a numerical value up to 5 written on them. Put all the cards into a 'feely' bag. The children should play a game where they take a card from the bag, read the word and spell its singular or plural equivalent. If the others agree they are correct, they win points to the value on their card. The winner is the child with the highest tally at the end of the game.

4 Give the children copies of Generic sheet 2 (page 119) with some 'consonant + y' words and some 'ies' words. They should use them to help them to learn to spell the words using the 'Look, Say, Cover, Write, Check' strategy.

Plenary session

■ Ask the children to tell you as many 'y' words as they can to beat an egg-timer. When the sand runs through, let each child who gave you a correct word come out and write their word on the board. Turn the egg-timer over and see if others can tell you the plurals before the sand runs through. Play the game in reverse.

■ Is everybody quite sure about how to make the plural of a word ending in 'consonant + y'? Did they enjoy their activities? Was there anything they found difficult?

■ Remind them that there are some words that end in 'y' that have a different rule for turning them into plurals. Can anyone remember one of the words? (monkey, valley and so on)

■ Which of these points help to make a story exciting? Tick the
ones you agree with.

Short, quick words that move the action on ☐

Gentle, quiet dialogue ☐

A slow pace ☐

Powerful and imaginative words ☐

A series of events told quickly ☐

Fast, tense dialogue ☐

A calm setting ☐

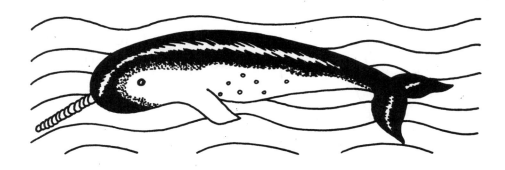

■ Choose your favourite part of *Why the Whales Came* and
write a few of the exciting words on the back of this sheet.

■ Write a few sentences about why you think it was an
exciting part of the story.

■ Write what the people said as reported speech.

_____

_____

■ Read these sentences and write in the speech bubbles
what the people said.

The girl said she forgot to do
her homework.

The teacher told the children to
sit down and be quiet.

■ Write this as reported speech.

The man said, 'I have to go to work now.'

_____

■ Write this as direct speech.

Rick said he was going to play football.

_____

■ Write the plural of these words. One has been done for you.

story → _____stories_____   baby → _____

body → _____   jelly → _____

lady → _____   family → _____

■ Write the singular of these words. One has been done for you.

countries → ___country___   armies → _____

spies → _____   carries → _____

worries → _____   stories → _____

■ Find all the words in this wordsearch.

a	r	m	i	s	e	i	d	o	b
r	s	a	m	b	a	b	y	k	a
m	t	r	f	a	m	x	p	s	b
f	a	m	i	l	i	e	s	y	i
y	i	y	j	e	l	l	i	m	e
e	s	r	s	e	i	r	o	t	s
w	o	r	r	y	r	o	t	s	j
b	a	a	y	s	e	i	d	a	l
i	e	c	o	u	n	t	r	y	y
j	e	l	l	i	e	s	y	i	e

ladies ←
spy ↑
families →
army ↓
stories ←
carry ↑
babies ↓
worry →
bodies ←
country →
story ←
jellies →

Stories and description

Overall aims

- To consider how description is used to effect in stories.
- To identify and classify 1st, 2nd and 3rd persons in a text.
- To explore synonyms.

Featured book

The Wizard of Oz by L Frank Baum, (many editions available)

Story synopsis

Dorothy is swept away from her home on the Kansas prairie by a cyclone and finds herself, with her little dog Toto, in a strange land among strange characters. Desperate to return to Aunt Em and Uncle Henry, she sets off to the City of Emeralds to find Oz, the Great Wizard who will help her to go home. On her way she meets up with a scarecrow who wants 'a brain', a tin man who wants a heart and a lion who wants courage. They travel together, meeting many strange, frightening and wonderful, as well as fierce and terrifying, characters. After many adventures, they arrive and each gets their dearest wish.

Lesson One

Intended learning

- To use the chosen text to illustrate good use of description.
- To consider how description is used to effect in the story.

With the whole class

Work on the first chapter will take one session. To complete the whole book may take several sessions.

- Tell the children that you are going to read the first chapter of *The Wizard of Oz* to them. Ask them to listen carefully to the descriptions. Read the first chapter and then discuss it together. What was Dorothy's house like? Were they able to visualise it? How could they do this? Write key words on the board that the children offer to describe the house, such as 'small', 'wooden', 'one room' and 'rusty stove'. Read the first paragraph again and as you reach a word that is on the board, tick it. What makes the description so graphic? Explain that the author has used simple and clear words in uncomplicated sentences which help us to visualise the scene.

- Ask volunteers to come and write on the board a word that describes the prairie. These might include 'grey', 'huge', 'flat', 'cracks' and 'grass'. Read the second paragraph again and compare how many of the words were remembered by the children. Encourage them to tell you how the descriptions helped them imagine the prairie. Can we visualise the prairie even if we haven't been there? How?

- Explain to the children that they are going to do some work on descriptions in the first chapter of the book before reading the rest of the book.

With the lower-achievers

With adult support

Choose from:

1. Ask the children why we use descriptive words. Help them to understand that descriptive words are more graphic and help us to imagine something more clearly. Ask them to describe what they are wearing and help them to use description to give a fuller picture. For example, 'Martin's jumper is the colour of tomatoes, knitted with a coarse, chunky texture and has a high neck.' Help them to use descriptive words to write about their favourite clothes such as a football kit or a special disco-dress.

2. Give out copies of Resource sheet 2a. Help the children to add descriptive words to complete the passage.

3. Give the children copies of Generic sheet 1 (page 118). Together discuss the story and agree the different descriptive words that could be used for each picture. They should make the story as effective as possible by the use of descriptions. What is the good fairy like? What is the wicked fairy like? Describe the attic.

4   Find a picture of an amazing creature, for example, and together agree a description. Stretch their vocabulary skills for this – *"Come on, give me an even better word than 'enormous'."* – and record the description on a cassette. Now read a prepared description of another amazing creature and ask the children to draw and label it according to your description.

Teacher-independent activities

Choose from:

1   Give the children copies of Resource sheet 2a to complete. They could work in pairs for support. You may need to read the sheet with them before letting them work independently.

2   Have prepared a set of cards with a descriptive word written on each. Let the children play a game where the cards are placed in a pile face down on the table. They should take a card, read it and add a suitable noun. For example, if they pick 'enormous' they could say 'elephant'. If the others agree, they win a token. The winner has the highest number of tokens at the end of the game.

3   Give the children copies of Generic sheet 1 (page 118). Ask them to work in pairs to find descriptive words for the story and write them on or near the pictures. They should use a dictionary and thesaurus to help them.

Plenary session

■   Read the second chapter of *The Wizard of Oz*. When you have finished ask the children if they can remember any descriptive passages you have just read. For example, what was the land of the Munchkins like? (Beautiful, green, rich, luscious fruits and gorgeous flowers.) What did the Munchkins look like? (As small as Dorothy but very old and wearing old clothes.)

Working with the whole book

■   Tell the children you are going to read the rest of the book over the next few weeks and that they should try to remember any descriptions they think are particularly good. At the end of each reading session, spend a few moments

discussing which passages they thought had good descriptions. Can they say why? Explore the vocabulary and the syntax together and discuss how the author uses these to effect. For example, in Chapter 12 (the description of the Winged Monkeys answering the call of the Wicked Witch), there are phrases such as 'a low rumbling sound', 'a great chattering and laughing' and 'a pair of immense and powerful wings', all being effective and powerful images which describe the event graphically.

■   When you have finished the book, discuss which parts were the children's favourites and why. Ask for volunteers to describe the fantasy creatures from memory and then check the text to see how accurate they were. Encourage the children to consider why they were able to describe the creatures. Explain that effective descriptions can make a lasting impression.

■   Ask the children to choose one of the fantasy creatures from the story. For example, the Munchkins, the Kalidahs or the Winged Monkeys. Help them to write a description of the creature. Tell them they will have the chance to read their descriptions at the plenary session and see if the others can identify the creature from their description.

Lesson Two

Intended learning

■   To identify and classify 1st, 2nd and 3rd persons in a text.

■   To use the chosen text as a basis for this.

■   To explore other texts for examples of 1st, 2nd and 3rd person.

With the whole class

■   Reread Chapter One or Chapter Two of *The Wizard of Oz*. When you have finished, ask the children what they think personal pronouns are (I, you, he, she, it, we, you and they). Ask for volunteers to come and write them on the board. Do the children know which are singular and which plural? Explain that these pronouns are referred to as '1st person', '2nd person' and '3rd person', 'singular' or 'plural' as appropriate.

- Divide the board into halves, headed 'singular' and 'plural'. Ask for a volunteer to write each pronoun in the correct column. Then ask somebody else to mark each as 1st, 2nd or 3rd person. What do they notice about 'you'?

- Ask the children if they can remember which pronouns were in the chapter you have just read from *The Wizard of Oz*. Find some of them and read them out again. Write them on the board with their owner: 'She' – 'Dorothy', 'He' – 'Toto', 'It' – 'the cyclone/house' and so on.

With the lower-achievers

With adult support

Choose from:

1. Make sure the children fully understand what the personal pronouns are, what singular and plural are and what the 1st, 2nd and 3rd person categories are. If necessary, spend more time going through some favourite stories helping them to find examples. Together make a large illustrated chart with the pronouns and their owners from *The Wizard of Oz*, which shows, for example, an illustration of Dorothy and the word 'she'.

2. Using Resource sheet 2b help the children to match the pronouns to their category. They should then write a sentence for each picture making sure they use the correct pronoun. Challenge them to write sentences on the back of the sheet for the pronouns they did not use.

3. Divide the hall or the playground into halves, 'Singular' and 'Plural', each with an area labelled '1st', '2nd' and '3rd'. Play a game where everybody stands in the centre and you call out a pronoun. The children should run to the correct part of the area. For example, if you call out *"she"*, the children should run to the area labelled 'Singular' and stand in the '3rd' person section. Make sure there is no pressure here and that the children enjoy the game for itself.

Teacher-independent activities

Choose from:

1. Give the children copies of Resource sheet 2b to complete.

2. Using Generic sheet 3 (page 120) make the spinning top and set of pronoun cards by sticking the sheet onto card and cutting out the shapes. You could make an extra set of pronoun cards if more are needed. Let the children play a game where they take turns to spin the top. They take the correct pronoun card according to how the top finished spinning and then say a sentence with the pronoun. The sentence could be from any story or from the story shown on Generic sheet 1. If the others agree they are correct, they win a token. The winner has the highest number of tokens at the end.

Plenary session

- Does everybody understand how personal pronouns are classified? Ask for volunteers to tell you. Can they write them on the board?

- Copy Generic sheet 1 onto acetate and show it on the OHP. Ask for volunteers in turn to tell the story, using pronouns only – no names, such as 'the princess'. Demonstrate this for them. For example, for the first picture say 'She was waving a wand over her.' Agree that we can't use pronouns all the time!

Lesson Three

Intended learning

- To revise synonyms and use the term 'synonym' correctly.

- To use the chosen text as a basis for exploring synonyms.

With the whole class

- Write on the board 'shouted', 'yelled', 'cried', 'squealed' and 'bawled'. Read these with the children. Ask them to tell you what they have in common. Encourage them to add some more words to the list.

■ Write 'synonyms' on the board and ask for a volunteer to read it. What does it mean? Remind the children of the work they did in Years 3 and 4 on synonyms. Tell them that the words you have written are synonyms.

■ Invite the children to give you some words to start 'synonym groups' or start them off yourself with examples such as 'big', 'funny' or 'saw'. Together, brainstorm as many synonyms for each word as possible. Encourage them to use dictionaries and thesauruses to find more. Let them write the words on the board. For example, for 'big' they might write 'large', 'enormous', 'huge', 'gigantic' and so on.

■ Look at the first sentence in *The Wizard of Oz*. 'Dorothy lived in the midst of the great Kansas prairies, with Uncle Henry, who was a farmer, and Aunt Em, who was the farmer's wife.' Ask the children which word could be added to the list of synonyms for 'big' (great). Ask for volunteers to choose words from the text that could be used as the first word of a synonym group. Again, use the dictionaries and thesauruses. List the synonyms and leave them on the board while working on this lesson.

With the lower-achievers

With adult support

Choose from:

1 Prepare cards with a 'start word' written on each, perhaps this time using 'feelings' words such as 'happy'. Make sure there is a dictionary and a thesaurus for at least each pair of children. Put the cards in a 'feely' bag and let the children take one card at a time. Help them to use the dictionary and thesaurus to find synonyms for the word on their card. They should write a list with the 'start word' at the top in a different colour. Encourage them to create verbal sentences using their synonyms.

2 Give out copies of Resource sheet 2c. Encourage the children to use the dictionary and thesaurus to complete the sheet.

3 Give out copies of Generic sheet 1 (page 118). Together tell the story and list as many

synonyms as possible for each picture. For example, for 'good' fairy there is 'kind', 'nice' and so on.

Teacher-independent activities

Choose from:

1 Give the children copies of Generic sheet 1 (page 118). Tell them to think about the different characters in the story. In pairs, they should choose two of the characters, write their names on a sheet of paper and a word to describe them. They then use a dictionary and thesaurus to find two synonyms for each of the words. They then find words that are complete opposites, so for 'good' fairy they find the words 'wicked', 'evil', 'bad' and so on.

2 Give the children copies of Resource sheet 2c to complete. They could work in pairs for support.

3 Give the children the list of words from the Medium Frequency Word List in the *National Literacy Strategy Framework*. They should write some of the words at the top of a card and then use a dictionary and thesaurus to find as many synonyms for them as possible.

Plenary session

■ Play a game of 'Quick-fire Synonyms'. Call out a word from *The Wizard of Oz* or Generic sheet 1 (page 118) and ask the children to reply with a synonym as quickly as possible. What is the maximum number of words found in a minute? Encourage them to beat their own record.

■ Ask a volunteer to tell you what 'synonym' means. Where can we find synonyms? (dictionaries and thesauruses)

■ Finish these sentences about The Wizard of Oz. Use the descriptive words in the box below to help you.

The prairie where Dorothy lived was _____

_____

During the cyclone, the wind _____

_____

Toto was Dorothy's dog and he was _____

_____

The sun and wind changed Aunt Em. She was now _____

_____

huge	dry	howled	everywhere	
flat	blew	hard	pretty	thin
grey	grass	roared	gaunt	twinkling eyes
cracked	blasted	serious	little	silky coat

■ On the back of this sheet, write a description of the house during the cyclone.

■ Match the pronouns to the right person. (One has been done for you.)

I	3rd person singular
it	2nd person plural
he	1st person singular
you	3rd person plural
we	2nd person singular
she	3rd person singular
they	1st person plural
you	3rd person singular

■ Write a sentence for each picture. Remember to use the correct pronouns and verbs.

_____

_____

_____

_____

_____

_____

_____

_____

■ Write some sentences on the back of this sheet for the pronouns you didn't use.

■ Put the synonyms in the right boxes.

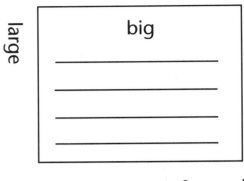

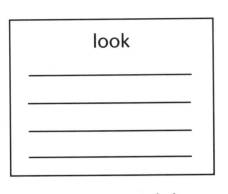

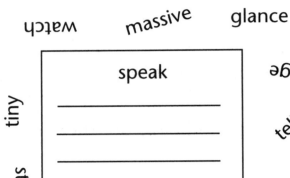

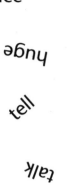

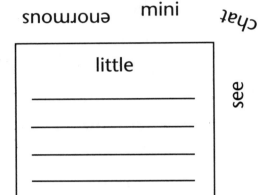

■ Find the synonyms for these words. Use a thesaurus or dictionary to help you.

light	pull

good	shut

Stories and story openings

Overall aims

- To explore and compare a range of story openings.

- To revise and extend work on verb tenses.

- To investigate the spelling rule that changes 'f' to 'ves'.

Featured books

The Farthest-Away Mountain by Lynne Reid Banks, Collins, 1988

The Headless Ghost by Pete Johnson, A & C Black, 1998

Story synopses

In *The Farthest-Away Mountain*, Dakin has three ambitions: to visit the farthest-away mountain (which nobody has ever reached), to meet a gargoyle and to marry a prince. The book recounts the trials and adventures she goes through to achieve these dreams, in a fairytale genre that goes beyond the usual.

The Headless Ghost tells of Grant's fear on seeing the headless ghost of an RAF officer at the war memorial. Grant is compelled to return to the memorial, though, and to try to work out what the ghost is saying. He eventually realises that it is warning of an unexploded bomb nearby. The bomb is located and made safe, and Grant becomes the local hero. The ghost is never seen again.

Lesson One

Intended learning

- To compare and discuss the openings of the two chosen texts.

- To express and justify an opinion about the openings.

With the whole class

- Tell the children you are going to read the first parts of two books and that afterwards they are going to compare the openings. Show the covers of the books and ask the children what they think the stories might be about. Do they think the books are going to be similar or different? Why?

- Read the preface of *The Farthest-Away Mountain* and then the first chapter of *The Headless Ghost*, letting the children see the illustrations from *The Headless Ghost*.

- Discuss the openings together. Ask the children where and when the stories are set. How do they know? What kinds of stories do they think they are going to be – fantasy, science fiction, historical? Why do they think this? Ask them what the differences are between the two openings (3rd person/1st person narrative; historical/modern settings; set in Britain/abroad, probably the Alps; no illustrations/comic-strip style; fairytale genre/the paranormal). Which opening do they prefer? Why? Do the openings make them want to read on? Why or why not?

With the lower-achievers

With adult support

Choose from:

1 Explore both openings again with the children and discuss some of the points that were raised in the whole-class session. Encourage them to say what they think is going to happen next in each story and why. How did each opening make them feel? Which book do they think is the more interesting? Encourage the children to give reasons for their answers. Help them to write about which opening they prefer and why. Help them to use dictionaries for words they are not sure how to spell.

2 Give the children copies of Resource sheet 3a. They should read the statements about the chosen texts and then write the numbers in the correct boxes. Give reading support if necessary.

3 Provide a selection of other books. Read and discuss the openings of each one. Explore the narration, the setting, style, genre and so on. The children should choose their favourite opening and say why. They could share this with the others during the plenary session. Perhaps that opening could be read then.

4   Give the children copies of Generic sheet 4 (page 121). Help them to read the openings on the sheet and discuss which they prefer and why. Help them to make notes about each one.

Teacher-independent activities

Choose from:

1   Give the children copies of Resource sheet 3a to complete. You may need to read it through with them before letting them work independently. They could work in pairs for support.

2   Ask the children to work in pairs to choose a well-known story, such as Superman or Star Wars. Give them a copy of Generic sheet 5 (page 122). Ask them to plan the story and then write the opening paragraph. This should be exciting enough to make the reader want to finish the story. If writing is too difficult, they could record their opening onto a cassette.

3   Have prepared a sheet of paper with a chart with the following headings: 'Time', 'Place', '1st/3rd person' and 'Type'. Give the children copies of Generic sheet 4 (page 121). They should read the openings on the sheet and complete the chart.

Plenary session

■   Let the children who chose a favourite opening read it to the others and say why they liked it. Do the others agree?

■   Ask the children who wrote openings for a well-known story to read these aloud to the class. The children who recorded their openings onto a cassette can play them to the others.

Lesson Two

Intended learning

■   To revise and extend work on verb tenses.

■   To use the chosen texts as a basis for working on verbs.

With the whole class

■   Divide the board into three sections headed 'past tense', 'present tense' and 'future tense'. Ask some of the children what they are doing just now. They may give answers such as 'I am sitting down', 'I am listening to you' or 'I am thinking.' Challenge them to tell you which tense they are speaking in. Agree it is the present tense. Remind them of the work they did in Year 4 on verbs and verb tenses.

■   Give the children a statement in the present tense and ask them what it would be in the past tense. ('I sat down/was sitting down'; 'I listened/was listening'; 'I thought/was thinking.') Ask other children for the future tense. ('I shall/will sit down', 'I shall/will listen' and 'I shall/will think.')

■   Ask for volunteers to come and write some verbs on the board, for example 'jump', 'play', 'look', 'kick' and 'shout'. Play 'Speed Tenses' against the clock. Ask different children to give one of the verbs in a specified tense. If they answer correctly they come and tick the board in the right section. How many ticks can the children accumulate in, say, a minute? The game will be fast and noisy!

■   Look at pages 11, 17 and 46 of *The Headless Ghost* for examples of the future tense in the contracted form ('I'll' and so on). Encourage the children to give some more examples. Let them write them on the board.

■   Read a page from *The Farthest-Away Mountain*. Stop after you have said each verb and ask the children to tell you what tense it is. They should get quicker and quicker at this!

With the lower-achievers

With adult support

Choose from:

1   Prepare two sets of cards. One set should have a noun written on each and the other set should have a verb and a tense written on each. For example, 'dog' and 'sing – future tense'. Put the sets of cards into separate 'feely' bags. The children take a card from each bag, read the words and then make the sentence. For example, 'The dog will sing.' The sentences can be nonsense. Encourage the children to write the funniest examples.

2   Using Resource sheet 3b, help the children to fill in the gaps on the snail's shell with the different verb tenses. They should then complete the table of contracted future tenses.

3   Write some verbs in the left-hand column of Generic sheet 6 (page 123), such as 'jump', 'play', 'work', 'shout' and 'laugh'. Help the children to complete the table with the correct words for each column. They should use dictionaries to help them.

4   Cut out the verb cards on Generic sheet 7 (page 124). Place them in a pile face down on the table. The children should take a card and tell you all the tenses of the verb depicted in the picture.

Teacher-independent activities

Choose from:

1   Give the children copies of Resource sheet 3b to complete.

2   Prepare a set of cards with 'Past', 'Present' or 'Future' written on each – at least four of each. Copy and cut out Generic sheet 7 (page 124). Place both sets of cards face down. You also need a 'Draughts' board and enough draughtsmen for each child to have one. The draughtsmen should be lined up on one side of the board. The children should take a verb card and a tense card and tell the others the correct tense of the verb depicted in the picture. If the others agree they are right, they move their draughtsman forward one space. The winner is the first to arrive at the other side of the board.

3   Write several verbs in the left-hand column of Generic sheet 6 (page 123) or let the children work in pairs to choose some verbs from Generic sheet 7 (page 124) and write them in the left-hand column. The children should complete the chart with the correct tenses of the verbs. They should use dictionaries to help them.

Plenary session

■   Does everybody understand what 'verb tense' means? Is everybody sure of the past tense, the present tense and the future tense? Was there anything difficult that needs to be explored a little further?

■   Lead the whole class in retelling a well-known story in a different tense. For example, 'Once upon a time' becomes 'One day soon' or 'Today'. 'Jack climbed the beanstalk' becomes 'Jack will climb the beanstalk' or 'Jack is climbing the beanstalk.' Give the children time to come up with the different tenses – it's not always as easy as it sounds!

Lesson Three

Intended learning

■   To investigate the spelling rule that changes 'f' to 'ves'.

■   To practise applying this rule.

With the whole class

Before the lesson prepare a set of cards, half with a noun ending in 'f' written on each and half with a noun ending in 'ves'. Put all the cards in a 'feely' bag.

■   Ask the children to tell you some nouns that end with 'f'. Write them on the board. You could give them a start with 'wolf' and 'shelf'. They may well suggest words that will prove an exception to the rule, such as 'chief', 'cliff', 'roof' and 'staff'. Write those exceptions on the board but to one side of the others. Now ask them for the plural of 'wolf' (or another word they suggested). Ask for volunteers to come and write the plurals beside the singulars. Has everybody noticed what happened to the 'f'? Draw a clear line between the body of the word and the final 'f' and write 'ves' beside it in a different colour.

■ Explain that there are always exceptions to rules and that the words ending with 'f' that you wrote to one side of the board do not comply with the rule of a word ending with 'f' having a plural of 'ves'.

■ Now write on the board 'halves', 'leaves', 'thieves' and 'calves'. Ask for volunteers to come and write the singular of each word. Did they remember to change the 'ves' to 'f'?

■ Ask for volunteers to 'Go Fishing'. They should come and fish in the 'feely' bag for a card and read it. Challenge them to write on the board the singular or plural of the word.

With the lower-achievers

With adult support

Choose from:

1 Make sure the children understand that the final 'f' is changed to 'ves' for the plural of many words that end in 'f'. Play 'Quick Fire'. Say a word (with either an 'f' or 'ves' ending) and ask for the singular or plural. How many words can they say or spell correctly while an egg-timer is running? Challenge them to beat their own score.

2 Give out copies of Resource sheet 3c. Help the children to write the singular or plural of the words in the oval shapes. They should then complete the crossword.

3 Give the children copies of Generic sheet 2 (page 119) with some 'f' and 'ves' words. Help them to learn to spell the words using the 'Look, Say, Cover, Write, Check' strategy.

Teacher-independent activities

Choose from:

1 Let the children work in pairs to complete Resource sheet 3c.

2 Ask the children to make a word wall with 'f' and 'ves' words in each 'brick'. Tell them that the singular and the plural of each word should be in adjoining 'bricks'. They can add to the wall whenever they find new words.

3 Give the children copies of Generic sheet 2 (page 119) with some 'f' and 'ves' words written in. Let them work in pairs and learn to spell the words using the 'Look, Say, Cover, Write, Check' strategy.

Plenary session

■ Tell the children you want them to tell you as many words that end in 'f' as they can while an egg-timer runs. When the sand runs through, let each child who gave you a correct word come out and write their word on the board. Turn the egg-timer over and see if others can tell you the plurals before the sand runs through. Play the game in reverse.

■ Is everybody quite sure about how to make the plural of a word ending in 'f'? Is everybody quite sure about how to make the singular of a word ending in 'ves'?

Name _____

■ Read these statements about the two books you have read and write the number of each statement in the correct box below.

1. This book is written in the first person.

2. This book is set in modern times.

3. This book is a fairytale.

4. This book is set in Britain.

5. This book has just a few pictures.

6. This book is like a comic.

7. This book is set in a foreign country.

8. This book is a ghost story.

9. This book has an historical setting.

10. This book is written in the third person.

The Farthest-Away Mountain						

The Headless Ghost						

■ Which book do you prefer? _____

■ Why? _____

_____

■ Write about the openings of two more books on the back of this sheet.

■ Go round the snail's shell writing the past, present and future tenses for each verb. The first one has been done for you.

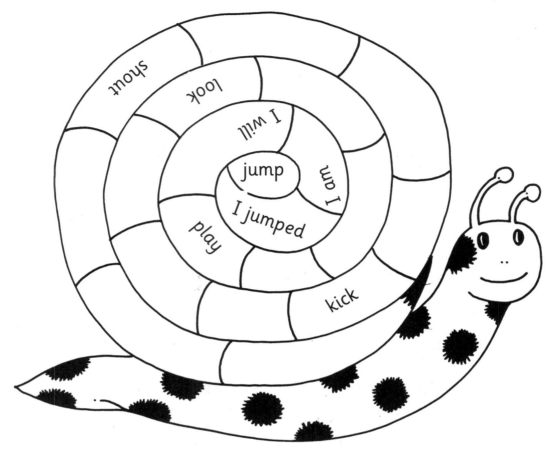

■ Shorten these future tenses as in the example.

I shall work ➤ I'll work

I shall jump ➤ _____

I will play ➤ _____

I will shout ➤ _____

■ Write all the tenses on the back of the sheet for these words (but be careful).

laugh   sing   think

■ Write the singular or plural in the empty shapes.

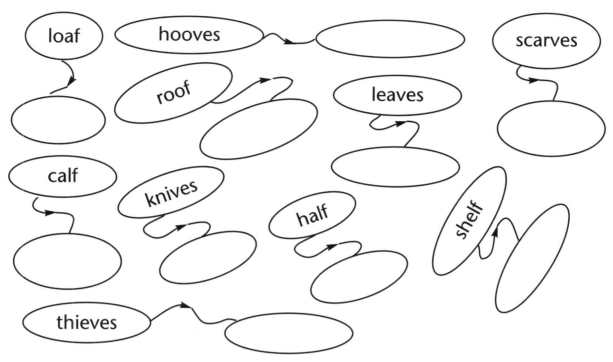

■ Complete the crossword.

ACROSS

2 People who steal.

4 Two equal parts of a whole thing.

6 Large pieces of bread.

8 The top of a house.

9 A horse's foot.

DOWN

1 A baby cow.

3 You keep books on these.

5 They fall off the trees in autumn.

7 This keeps your neck warm in winter.

Poems by significant poets

Overall aims

- To explore poems by the same poet.
- To identify what is distinct about the content and style of the poems.
- To use the poetry as a stimulus to read other poems by the same poet and other significant poets.

Featured books

A First Poetry Book compiled by John Foster, Oxford University Press, 1979 (1989 edition)

The Puffin Book of Utterly Brilliant Poetry edited by Brian Patten, Puffin Books, 1998

Lesson One

Chosen poems

'When we go over to my grandad's' and 'Who Started It?' by Michael Rosen, page 31

Intended learning

- To explore poems by the same poet.
- To identify what is distinct about the content and style of the poems.
- To use the poetry as a stimulus to write own poems.
- To use the poetry as a stimulus to read other poems by the same poet.

With the whole class

- Enlarge copies of 'When we go over to my grandad's' and 'Who Started It?' Tell the children that these are poems by the same poet, Michael Rosen, and you are going to explore together what they are about and how they are written.
- Read 'When we go over to my grandad's', letting the children follow the text. What is the poem about? Do any of the children have a grandad who falls asleep and snores? When he wakes up, does he ask 'Was I snoring?' and

what do they say? Who else could this poem have been about? Why do the children in the poem lie to their grandad?

- Explore the structure and style of the poem. How many verses are there? How many lines are in each verse? Is there a regular verse pattern? How do they know? Does the poem rhyme? Does it have a regular rhythm?

- Read 'Who Started It?' letting the children follow the text. What is this poem about? How is the content similar to 'When we go over to my grandad's'? Point out that both poems are about families. Do the children recognise the situation in the poem? Do they argue about who starts fights at home? Ask them to consider whether this poem could have been written about someone else, such as friends.

- Explore the structure and style of the poem. Again, ask how many verses there are, how many lines there are in each verse and whether the poem rhymes. Does it have a regular rhythm? What are the similarities of style and structure between the two poems? The children should mention things such as the poems don't have a rhyming pattern, they don't have a regular verse pattern and they don't have a regular rhythm. List the points they make on the board and leave them up while working on this lesson.

- Did the children enjoy the poems? Encourage them to give reasons for their answers. Tell the children that we don't always like every poem we read and that a negative opinion is as valid and valued as a positive one – there are no 'rights and wrongs' to poetry. Which of the two is their favourite? Why?

With the lower-achievers

With adult support

Choose from:

1 Revisit both poems and discuss together how they are similar in style and content. Look at the list written on the board during the whole-class session. Help the children to write some sentences about the poems' style and structure. Ask them to write a few sentences about which is their favourite and why.

2   Using Resource sheet 4a, help the children to read the statements about the two poems. They should identify the similarities and tick the appropriate boxes. Give reading support where necessary.

3   Explore more of Michael Rosen's poetry. Choose two or three poems to read together and compare them with 'When we go over to my grandad's' and 'Who Started It?' Draw up a chart with the following headings: 'rhymes', 'doesn't rhyme', 'regular rhythm', 'no regular rhythm', 'regular verse pattern', 'no regular verse pattern'. Let the children look at the list on the board to jog their memories. Help them to analyse the rhyme, rhythm and verse patterns (regular or irregular) of the poems you explore and complete the chart.

4   Give the children copies of Resource sheet 4b and help them to write a poem about a fight with their brother or sister. They can use the words on the sheet or choose their own. Challenge them to write another verse independently.

Teacher-independent activities

Choose from:

1   Ask the children to choose one of the poems to practise a role-play. Tell them they should try to incorporate at least one line of dialogue from the poem into the play, such as 'No, you didn't snore,' or 'Stoppit [sic] – someone'll get hurt.'

2   Cut up 'When we go over to my grandad's' into verses. Challenge the children to first put the verses in the wrong order and read them aloud and then put the verses back into the correct order and read it aloud again. They could work in pairs to do this.

3   Ask the children to think about someone they visit and the things that person does. Can they write a few lines about it? They could use a dictionary and thesaurus to help them and illustrate the writing with a picture of the person.

Plenary session

- Ask the children who practised a role-play to give a performance for the class. Did they remember to use one line of dialogue from their chosen poem?

- Ask the children if any of them would like to read their own poem or one of Michael Rosen's to the class.

Lesson Two

Chosen poem

'Going Through the Old Photos' by Michael Rosen, page 32

Intended learning

- To continue exploring poems by the same poet.

- To identify what is distinct about the content and style of the poems.

- To use the poetry as a stimulus to explore the work of other significant poets.

With the whole class

- Enlarge a copy of 'Going Through the Old Photos'. Also have ready a selection of poems by two or three other significant poets such as Roger McGough, Benjamin Zephaniah or Jack Prelutsky.

- Ask the children to remember the names of the poems and the poet they explored in Lesson One. Tell them they are going to read another of Michael Rosen's poems. Read the poem with them, letting them follow the text. Ask them what the poem is about. Have they ever looked through old photos at home and asked who everybody is?

- Explore the structure and style of the poem. How many verses are there? How many lines are in each verse? Ask the children if there is a regular verse pattern (most verses have four lines). Point out that the verse pattern isn't regular but it is more consistent than the other poems explored. Does the poem rhyme? Which words rhyme? Let the children come and write the rhyming words on the board. Does the poem have a regular rhythm?

- Do the children think the poem is similar to or different from the other Michael Rosen poems they have explored? Why? Is the theme or content similar or different? Ask them how they know this poem is also about families (by expressions such as Auntie Mabel, Uncle Billy, Uncle Ted and so on).

- Read one or two of the poems by other poets. Let the children enjoy the poems for their own sake without too much analysis. Which did they enjoy? Were there any they didn't like so much? Which poet would they like to explore further? Why?

With the lower-achievers

With adult support

Choose from:

1   Look again at all three Michael Rosen poems. Let the children choose their favourite and then help them to practise reciting it. If it is too long, take an extract and help them learn it. Encourage them to use intonation and expression to convey the mood of the poem.

2   Ask the children to complete Resource sheet 4c, referring to their favourite poem. Give reading support where necessary.

3   Together, explore some poems by two or three other poets. Discuss together which poems they enjoyed and why. Help the children to explore style, content and structure. Let them choose one each to share with the others during the plenary session.

Teacher-independent activities

Choose from:

1   Let the children work in pairs to complete Resource sheet 4c.

2   Prepare copies of 'Going Through the Old Photos' with the names of the people blanked out – for example,
    Who's that?
    That's…
    and that's…

Give them to the children and ask them to complete the lines to make a new poem. They could use their own names from their own families. Remind them that the poem doesn't have to rhyme and let them see the original for support.

3   Ask the children to work in pairs. Give them an anthology with work by other significant poets. If they find selecting from a full anthology too difficult, you could mark a selection of two or three poets and tell them to explore these. They should look at the poems together and choose one or two to share with the class. Let them record them onto a cassette.

Plenary session

- Ask the children who chose favourite poems by other writers to share these with the class. Why did they choose the poems? Let the children who made recordings play the cassette to the others.

- Ask the children who learned one of the poems to recite it to the class. Did they enjoy practising for their performance? Why did they choose that particular poem to learn?

- Ask the children who wrote their own versions of 'Going Through the Old Photos' to read them to the class.

When we go over to my grandad's

When we go over
to my grandad's
he falls asleep.

While he's asleep
he snores.

When he wakes up,
he says,
'Did I snore?
did I snore?
did I snore?'

Everybody says, 'No,
you didn't snore.'

Why do we lie to him?

Michael Rosen

Who Started It?

When me and my brother have a fight
my mum says:
'Stoppit – someone'll get hurt.'

And we say:
'He started it.'
'I didn't. He started it.'

I say:
'Mum, who started the very first fight
between me and Brian?'

And she says:
'You.'

'Me? But I'm four years younger than
    him.
How could it have been me?'

And she says:
'Well, it was like this . . .

You were about two years old
and Brian was six.
You were sitting in your high chair
eating your breakfast
and Brian walked past.
You leaned forward
and banged him over the head
with your spoon.'

'There you are,' says my brother,
'you started it,
you started it.
I always knew you started it.'

Michael Rosen

Going Through the Old Photos

Who's that?
That's your Auntie Mabel
and that's me under the table.

Who's that?
That's Uncle Billy.
Who's that?
Me being silly.

Who's that
licking a lolly?
I'm not sure
but I think it's Polly.

Who's that
behind the tree?
I don't know,
I can't see.
Could be you.
Could be me.

Who's that?
Baby Joe.
Who's that?
I don't know.

Who's that standing
on his head?
Turn it round.
It's Uncle Ted.

Michael Rosen

■ Read 'When we go over to my grandad's' and put a tick (✓) in the box if you agree with the sentence.

It has a regular verse pattern. ☐

It is about families. ☐   It rhymes. ☐

There is no regular rhythm. ☐

It does not have a regular verse pattern. ☐

It doesn't rhyme. ☐

■ Read 'Who Started It?' and put a tick (✓) in the box if you agree with the sentence.

It has a regular rhyming pattern. ☐

There is no regular rhythm. ☐ It's about school. ☐

It has an irregular verse structure. ☐

There are regular beats. ☐

It rhymes. ☐

It doesn't rhyme. ☐

■ Read 'Who Started It?' by Michael Rosen.

■ Write your own poem here. You can use the words at the bottom of the sheet to help you.

When _____ and I

Have a fight,

My _____ says

_____

And we say, _____

Then we _____

When _____

_____

_____

brother	teacher	laugh	cross
sister	Mum	shout	started
friend	Dad	quiet	funny

■ Write another verse on the back of the sheet.

■ Complete the following about your favourite poem by Michael Rosen.

What is the title of the poem?

_____

Does the poem use rhyme?   Yes ☐   No ☐

If yes, write two words from the poem that rhyme.

1. _____   2. _____

Does the poem have a regular verse pattern?   Yes ☐ No ☐

If yes, write how many lines. _____

What is the poem about? _____

_____

Does the poem have a regular rhythm?   Yes ☐ No ☐

Explain how you know this. _____

_____

_____

Write your favourite line from the poem.

_____

Why is it your favourite line?

_____

_____

Poems with word play

Overall aims

- To explore poems which have a play on words.
- To identify how the play on words relates to the meaning of the poem.
- To use the poetry as a stimulus for own work.

Featured book

The Puffin Book of Utterly Brilliant Poetry edited by Brian Patten, Puffin Books, 1998

Lesson One

Chosen poem

'On and on…' by Roger McGough, page 39

Intended learning

- To explore the play on words contained within the chosen poem.
- To identify other words or phrases that could be used for word play.

With the whole class

- Enlarge a copy of 'On and on…' Tell the children that this poem is by Roger McGough and it is about playing with words. What does 'playing with words' mean? Explain that many jokes and all puns work because of a play on words. Ask the children to tell some jokes. Pick out the jokes that rely on word play for effect and explore them together. 'Knock Knock' jokes are a good source.

- Read the poem to the children, allowing them to follow the text. Let them enjoy each of the puns and examples of word play. At the end, ask if there are any words or phrases that the children do not understand, such as 'opera buff', 'pony trap', 'bent copper' and so on. Explain these and read the poem again. This time, let the children join in.

- Encourage the children to think of some words that could be used for word play – for example, 'hand-bag' – a bag to put hands in; 'shoe-horn'

– a shoe played in an orchestra; 'egg-cup' – something an egg drinks from. Let the children come and write their words on a large sheet of paper. Challenge the class to guess what the play on the word is. Say they may add words to the list whenever they think of one or find one. Leave the sheet pinned on the wall together with a pen on a string.

With the lower-achievers

With adult support

Choose from:

1 Make sure the children understand what word play means and how it works. Share a few jokes and explore why they are funny. Read 'On and on…' again together, and discuss which phrases the children think are the funniest and why. Help them to make up some more word plays. They should write them in the style of 'On and on…' – for example, 'Is an armchair something your arm sits on?'

2 Using Resource sheet 5a, help the children to finish the verses with their own words. Challenge them to write one or two more verses on the back of the sheet, independently.

3 Give out copies of Resource sheet 5b. Ask the children to match each half of the verses and then write out each new verse. Challenge them to add some more verses of their own on the back of the sheet.

Teacher-independent activities

Choose from:

1 Give the children copies of Resource sheet 5a to complete. They may need to work in pairs to complete it.

2 Make a set of cards by sticking Resource sheet 5b onto card and cutting out the boxes. Mix the cards up and place them face down on the table. The children can play a form of 'Pelmanism' where they match up each half of the verses.

3 Let the children complete Resource sheet 5b. Again they may need to work in pairs. Read it through with them before letting them work independently.

Plenary session

■ Did any of the children add puns or word play to the list started during the whole-class session? Let them share these with the class.

■ Ask the children who wrote more verses for 'On and on...' to read these out to the class. Let the children who completed resource sheets or played a game explain what they had to do.

■ Ask for a volunteer to tell you what 'word play' means. Encourage the children to give you some examples.

Lesson Two

Chosen poem

'Gruesome' by Roger McGough, page 40

Intended learning

■ To explore the play on words and nonsense words in the chosen poem.

■ To identify how the nonsense words relate to the meaning of the poem.

■ To use the poetry as a stimulus for own work.

With the whole class

■ Enlarge a copy of 'Gruesome'. Tell the children they are going to explore another poem by Roger McGough which again has a play on words. Before reading the poem, ask a volunteer to look in the dictionary for the definition of 'gruesome'.

■ Read the poem with the children. Pause at the end and ask the children to supply the missing rhyme. How is this is a play on words? Ask how the final word(s) can be spelled ('gruesome' or 'grew some').

■ Ask the children what is meant by the line 'what is it ails thee so?' Explain how 'thee' is an old form of address that would often appear in ballads and that 'ails' means to trouble or bother.

■ Encourage guesses as to what a 'gruess' is. Remind the children of the work they did in Year 4 on gender words. What can they remember about the suffix 'ess'? Remind them it is for female words. Ask for some examples, such as 'princess', 'postmistress', 'air-hostess' and so on. Encourage them to tell you that a 'gruess' must be a female grue.

■ Do the children think 'grues' or 'gruesses' exist? Encourage them to give reasons for their answers. Explain how Roger McGough has made up a word in order to create the word play. Challenge the children to make up some nonsense words. Give them a start with examples: 'frog' and 'toad' could give 'froad' or 'grin' and 'smile' could give 'grile'. Let them come and write their new words on the board. Then invite them to create a silly sentence with the words, for example 'The froad hopped down the stroad ('street' and 'road').'

With the lower-achievers

With adult support

Choose from:

1 Read 'Gruesome' again with the children. Make sure they understand any words or phrases which they may have found difficult in the whole-class session. Ask them to tell you what the story is about. If necessary, explain again how there is a play on the word 'gruesome'. Do they know what the alternative is? ('Grew some') Allocate the dialogue to different children or partners and together practise reciting the poem, with you speaking the narrative parts. Help the children to use different voices and expression to show the different characters.

2 Ask the children if they can think of some words or phrases that could be used for word play – for example, 'kidney bean' could give 'kidney been', 'kid/knee'/'bean/been' and so on. Make a word wall with each of the new words and their play in a 'brick'. The wall can be added to and also be used as a stimulus for the children's own work. Help them to write a joke or pun for each of their words.

3 Using Resource sheet 5c, help the children to make up some new words from those on the

sheet. They should use these to write their own poems. Give support where necessary. Challenge them to make up some more of their own nonsense words and write them on the back of the sheet.

Teacher-independent activities

Choose from:

1   Using old newspapers, ask the children to cut up words from the headlines and make new nonsense words by pairing up different parts. For example, 'shock' and 'result' could give 'shult' or 'resock'. Challenge them to write silly sentences using their nonsense words.

2   Let the children complete Resource sheet 5c.

3   Ask the children to make a class joke book with puns, word play and nonsense words. Leave it available for the others to read and enjoy. You could put extra blank pages at the back and encourage the other children in the class to add to it.

Plenary session

■   Let the children who practised reciting 'Gruesome' give a class performance, with you reading the narrative parts.

■   Ask the children who made up nonsense words and used them to write sentences, to share these with the class. Ask the class to make different sentences using the same words.

■   Does everybody understand what we mean by word play, nonsense words and puns?

On and on...

Is a well-wisher someone
who wishes at a well?

Is a bad speller one who
casts a wicked spell?

Is a shop-lifter a giant who
goes around lifting shops?

Is a pop singer someone who
sings and then pops?

Is a pot-holer a gunman who
shoots holes at pots?

Does a baby-sitter really sit
on tiny tots?

Is a light bulb a bulb that is
as light as a feather?

Does an opera buff sing in
the altogether?

Does a pony trap trap ponies
going to the fair?

Is fire-hose stockings that
firemen wear?

Is a scratch team so itchy it
scratches?

When a bricklayer lays a brick
what hatches?

Is a sick bed a bed that is
feeling unwell?

Is a crime wave a criminal's
wave of farewell?

Is a bent copper a policeman
who has gone round the
bend?

Is the bottom line the line on
your bottom? THE END

Roger McGough

Gruesome

I was sitting in the sitting room
toying with some toys
when from a door marked:'GRUESOME'
there came a GRUESOME noise

Cautiously I opened it
and there to my surprise
a little GRUE sat sitting
with tears in its eyes

'Oh little GRUE please tell me
what is it ails thee so?'
'Well, I'm so small,' he sobbed,
'GRUESSES don't want to know.'

'Exercises are the answer,
each morning you must DO SOME.'
He thanked me, smiled,
and do you know what?
The very next day he ...

Roger McGough

■ Read 'On and on...' by Roger McGough. Write some more verses for the poem.

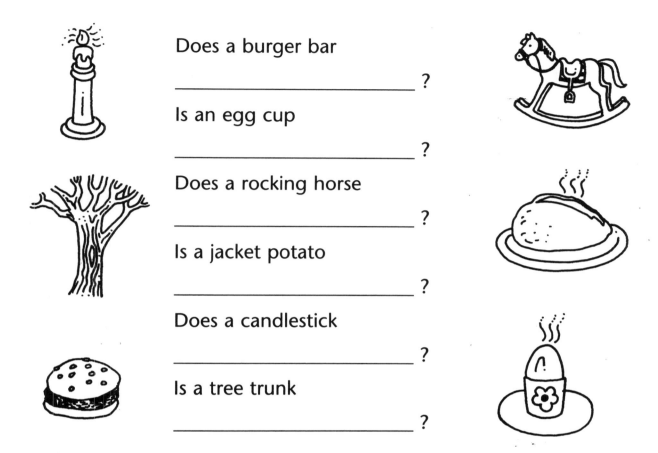

Does a burger bar

_____ ?

Is an egg cup

_____ ?

Does a rocking horse

_____ ?

Is a jacket potato

_____ ?

Does a candlestick

_____ ?

Is a tree trunk

_____ ?

■ Write some more verses here.

■ Match the halves to make more verses for 'On and on…'
by Roger McGough.

Is a crab apple	a shower for insects?
Is a pelican crossing	a hat for your oven?
Is fly spray	fruit for crabs?
Is a cooker hood	where roses sleep?
Is a flower bed	a bird going over the road?
Is a stainless steel sink	a bowl that won't float?

■ Write the verses out on the back of the sheet. Add some new
verses of your own.

■ Make some nonsense words from these.
A couple have been done for you.

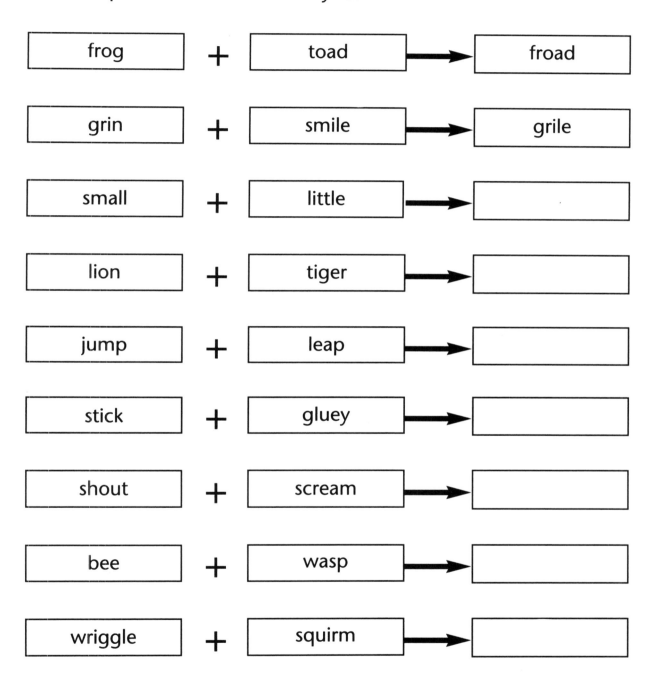

frog	+	toad	→	froad
grin	+	smile	→	grile
small	+	little	→	
lion	+	tiger	→	
jump	+	leap	→	
stick	+	gluey	→	
shout	+	scream	→	
bee	+	wasp	→	
wriggle	+	squirm	→	

■ Write some silly sentences with your new words on the back of this sheet. For example:

The froad hopped up a tree.

Stories with myths and legends

Overall aims

- To understand and use correctly the terms 'myth' and 'legend'.
- To identify the common features of myths and legends.
- To consolidate the agreement between nouns and verbs.
- To distinguish between homophones.

Featured book

The Orchard Book of Greek Myths by Geraldine McCaughrean, Orchard Books, 1992

Book synopsis

This collection of Greek myths covers the most famous stories such as Pandora's Box, King Midas, Jason and the Golden Fleece, and the The Wooden Horse of Troy. There are 16 stories in the collection, all of which are retold in a way that is clear and concise, at a level that the children can understand.

Lesson One

Intended learning

- To understand and use correctly the terms 'myth' and 'legend'.
- To identify the common features of myths and legends.

With the whole class

- Ask the children if they know what myths and legends are. Encourage them to name some, for example stories about giants, Robin Hood, dragons, the Minotaur, unicorns or King Arthur. List them on a large sheet of paper. Pin it on the wall and tell the children they may add to it as they find more examples.
- Say that you are going to read some Greek myths to them. Ask if any of them know when they were written. (c300BC) Spend a few moments explaining that in Ancient Greece these stories were an important part of their

culture. Read 'Pandora's Box' and 'The Wooden Horse of Troy'. Do the children think the stories have a special message? If so, what is it? Ask them whether they think the stories are true. Why or why not?

- Read several other myths and legends and then discuss them together. Some of the following points should be explored: some of the stories have animals, real and/or fantasy, as main characters and others have people; some are set in real locations, some in mythical places; some are to explain the origin of a 'truth', others to convey a moral; some have a theme such as trials and forfeits, good triumphing over evil and wisdom overcoming foolishness. Challenge the children to tell you which stories from *The Orchard Book of Greek Myths* are examples of each point.

- Explain the difference between a myth and a legend. A legend usually has a real human as the central character and the tales of their adventures have been embellished over time. A myth usually tells of gods or heroes and/or mythical creatures and often gives an explanation for some element of humans' life experiences.

- Decide together whether each of the tales you have read is a myth or a legend. Are some of them a mixture of the two? Look at the list drawn up during the earlier part of the session and decide together whether these are myths or legends, for example stories about giants are myths and Robin Hood is a legend.

With the lower-achievers

With adult support

Choose from:

1   Make sure the children understand the difference between a myth and a legend. Look again at the tales explored in the whole-class session and discuss together whether they are myths or legends. Let them choose an example of each from the featured book or from the list written during the whole-class session. Help them to write some sentences saying why their chosen tale is a myth or a legend.

2 Discuss together the myth or legend elements of 'Pandora's Box'. Give the children copies of Resource sheet 6a and help them to decide which statements are true. Give reading help where necessary. They should then complete the sentences about the actions of Pandora, Epimetheus and Zeus.

3 Discuss together some of the more recent stories and some that are closer to home, such as 'Big Foot', 'The Yeti', 'King Arthur' and 'William Tell'. Which are myths and which are legends? Encourage the children to give reasons for their conclusions. Challenge them to choose one of these stories and find out about it.

Teacher-independent activities
Choose from:

1 Ask the children to choose their favourite story from the featured book and practise a role-play. They should remember to include elements that make it a myth or a legend.

2 Give the children copies of Resource sheet 6a to complete in pairs. You may need to read it with them first.

3 Ask the children to work in pairs. Give them several sheets of A4 paper divided into four or six sections. They should retell their favourite myth from the featured book in cartoon form, using speech bubbles where they can. Remind them to include all the elements of a myth and to make sure that the story follows the correct sequence of events.

Plenary session

- Talk about people who are legendary, such as Robin Hood, and why they have become so. How many of their reported exploits are likely to be true?

- Discuss a modern-day person or one who lived recently who may in the future become a legendary character whose exploits are exaggerated. This might be a famous footballer or pop singer.

- Are there any modern-day myths? Do the children know about the Bermuda Triangle? Is the Loch Ness monster a myth?

Lesson Two

Intended learning
- To revise the terms 'noun' and 'verb'.
- To consolidate the agreement between nouns and verbs.

With the whole class
- Write a few nouns and verbs on the board. Ask the children to look at the lists and tell you what they are. Discuss the terms 'noun' and 'verb'. Ask for a few examples.

- Ask the children to give you some examples of nouns from the chosen text, for example 'troubles', 'fleece' and 'ears'. Challenge them to give you an associated verb for each noun. For example, 'fly' – 'the troubles flew out of Pandora's box,' 'find' – 'Jason sets off to find the golden fleece,' 'grow' – 'King Midas grew ears that were like an ass's.' Do their verbs agree with the nouns? Make sure, for example, that the child says, 'King Midas grew ears that were like an ass's,' not 'King Midas grew ears that was like an ass's.'

- Write several combinations of commonly used verbs on the board, such as 'see'/'sees', 'do'/'does', 'were'/'was' and 'is'/'are'. Ask the children for some nouns to go with these, making sure they agree, for example 'The cat sees the mouse.'

With the lower-achievers
With adult support
Choose from:

1 Together look through 'Pandora's Box' or 'Jason and the Golden Fleece' for examples of nouns and help the children to write them on the board. Ask them to put appropriate verbs with each noun, making sure they agree. Tell them the verbs don't necessarily have to come from the story.

2 Make a set of noun cards and a set of verb cards. Put each set into a separate box and play 'Lucky Dip'. Each child takes a card from each

box and makes the noun and verb agree. (The lottery of cards can lead to some examples that the children might find amusing – for example, 'worms sing'.)

3   Give out copies of Resource sheet 6b. Help the children to trace through the maze to the correct answer and then make the verb agree. Ask them to write sentences on the back of the sheet for the words at the bottom.

Teacher-independent activities

Choose from:

1   Make a set of noun cards and a set of verb cards and put each set into a separate box. The children take a card from each box and make the noun and verb agree. Challenge them to then write sentences with their selections. The sentences can be silly or nonsense, as long as the nouns and verbs agree.

2   Give the children copies of Resource sheet 6b to complete. You may need to read it with them first. They could work in pairs.

3   Prepare a cassette with examples of a noun and a verb together, such as 'the bird' and 'to sing'. Leave enough time between examples to allow the recorder to be switched on and off. Ask the children to work in pairs to decide how to make the noun and verb agree, for example 'The bird sings.' Encourage them to write their examples and try to expand them into a longer sentence, such as 'The bird sings in the tree.'

Plenary session

■   As a class play a noun and verb game. Organise the class into large groups and give each group a whiteboard to write on. Designate scribes. You call out a noun and the group quickly agrees a verb and writes it on their whiteboard. For example, you call out *"an aeroplane"* and they write 'flies' or 'soars' or 'lands'.

■   Play a silly version of the game where they have to write a verb that bears no relation to the noun. For example, you say *"an aeroplane"* and they write 'sings' or 'swims'. Make sure you include some plurals, such as 'flowers' or 'horses'.

Lesson Three

Intended learning

■   To understand and use correctly the term 'homophone'.

■   To distinguish between homophones.

With the whole class

■   Write on the board several examples of homophones such as 'cereal' and 'serial', 'flower' and 'flour' or 'bored' and 'board'. Ask for volunteers to read each pair. What do the words have in common? Tell the children that when two words sound the same, but are spelt differently, we call them 'homophones'.

■   Write 'homophone' on the board and read it with the children. Which word within it do they know? ('phone') Explain that the word 'homophone' is Greek and made up of two parts: 'homo' means 'the same' and 'phone' means 'sound' or 'voice'.

■   Invite the children to give you more examples. They may suggest 'eight'/'ate' or 'rain'/'rein'/ 'reign'. Let them come to the board to write their examples. Discuss together the spelling, meaning and pronunciation of each example.

■   Find some words in *The Orchard Book of Greek Myths* which are homophones. There are 'sea' ('see'), 'wait' ('weight') and so on. List them on a large sheet of paper and tell the children to add to it whenever they find more examples. Challenge them to find more than two of the same homophone, for example, 'rain', 'rein' and 'reign'.

With the lower-achievers

With adult support

Choose from:

1   Make sure the children fully understand the term 'homophone'. If necessary, spend some time going over the teaching points again until they have grasped it. Find more examples such as 'pain'/'pane', 'new'/'knew', 'blew'/'blue' and 'flee'/'flea'. Make a word wall, with each pair in

a 'brick'. Let the children add to it as they find more examples.

2   Using Resource sheet 6c, ask the children to join each pair of homophones. Give reading support if necessary. Then ask them to write a homophone for the words at the bottom of the sheet. Challenge them to find more pairs and write them on the back of the sheet.

3   Prepare a set of cards using Generic sheet 8 (page 125). Fold the cards over, separating the pairs of homophones. Play a game where two children are facing each other, one of them holds up a card to their partner and the partner reads the word and has to say a homophone for it. The first child then turns the card over to see if they were right. If they were was right, they take the next folded card; if not they have to try another homophone.

Teacher-independent activities

Choose from:

1   Give the children copies of Resource sheet 6c to complete in pairs for support.

2   Give the children copies of Generic sheet 8 (page 125) with one word of each pair blanked off. Challenge them to write a homophone for each example.

3   Prepare a set of cards using Generic sheet 8 (page 125). Cut the cards in two, separating the pairs of homophones. The children could play a form of 'Pelmanism' where the pairs are homophones.

Plenary session

■   Play a homophone game where you call out some words and the children have to call out the homophone. You might want to select children to suggest the homophone in order to give the lower-achievers a chance to participate.

■ Read 'Pandora's Box'. Circle the statements that are true.

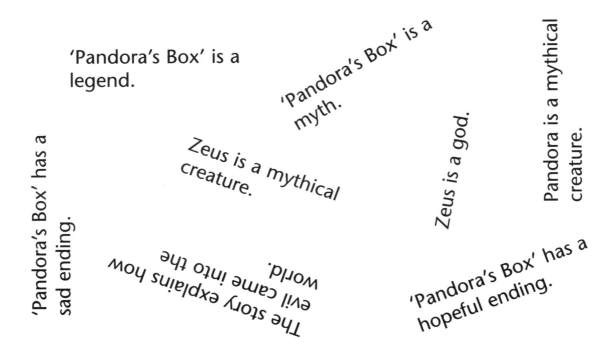

'Pandora's Box' is a legend.

'Pandora's Box' is a myth.

Zeus is a god.

Pandora is a mythical creature.

'Pandora's Box' has a sad ending.

Zeus is a mythical creature.

The story explains how evil came into the world.

'Pandora's Box' has a hopeful ending.

■ How do you think the characters in the story behaved? Finish these sentences.

Pandora was _____

_____

Zeus was _____

_____

Epimetheus was _____

_____

■ Choose the correct verb and put it into its sentence.
(You can follow the paths through the maze.)

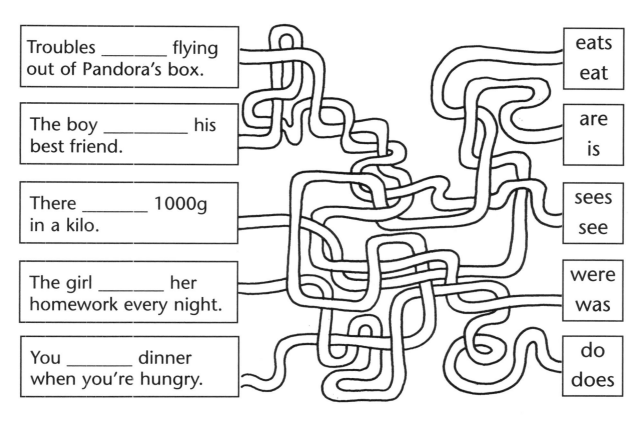

Troubles _____ flying out of Pandora's box.

The boy _____ his best friend.

There _____ 1000g in a kilo.

The girl _____ her homework every night.

You _____ dinner when you're hungry.

eats
eat

are
is

sees
see

were
was

do
does

■ Choose three of the verbs and write sentences for them.

_____

_____

_____

■ Choose one of these pairs of words. Write two sentences on the back of this sheet, one for each word.

look/looks   was/were   come/comes

■ Match these pairs of homophones. One has been done for you.

■ Write a homophone for these words.

cereal _____   bored _____

sea   _____   blue   _____

pair   _____   plain   _____

fowl   _____   flower _____

■ Find some more homophones and write them on the back of this sheet.

Stories with fables

Overall aims

■ To identify the features of a fable.

■ To consolidate the relationship between nouns and pronouns.

■ To investigate antonyms.

Featured book

Aesop's Fables compiled by Russell Ash and Bernard Higton, Pavilion Books, 1990

Book synopsis

The book has 53 fables and a detailed introduction about Aesop, the fables and the various versions of his fables over the centuries. Each fable is illustrated and is presented in a short format with the moral given at the end.

Lesson One

Intended learning

■ To identify the features of a fable.

■ To be stimulated to write own fable.

With the whole class

■ Ask the children if they can remember the work they did in Chapter 6 about the features of myths and legends. Tell them they are now going to explore some fables. Encourage them to name some fables. You could give them a start by suggesting 'The Hare and the Tortoise'.

■ Show them the cover of the book. Point out the name 'Aesop' and read it to them. Discuss the correct pronunciation ('ee–sop'). Tell the children who Aesop was, when and where he was supposed to have lived and how the fables have come down to us, originally orally and then written. You will find all this information in the featured edition of the fables.

■ Read three or four of the more familiar of Aesop's fables, for example 'The Lion and the Mouse', 'The Hare and the Tortoise' and 'The Fox and the Grapes'. Challenge the children to

identify some common features of the fables, for example a fable is usually a short story featuring an animal, the animal usually behaves like a human and the story is often amusing. List these and leave the list on the board while working on this lesson.

■ Tell the children that fables always have a 'moral'. Explain that a moral is a type of message told through the story about how generosity, loyalty and hard work get their own reward, or how good triumphs over evil. Read a definition of the word from a dictionary. Discuss what the moral is for each of the tales you have read. Add 'They always have a moral' to the list of common features of fables.

■ Ask the children to suggest some morals, for example 'Don't be greedy,' or 'We're all good at something.' List them on the board and leave the list up. Choose one of these morals and together make up a short story to illustrate it. Discuss whether it should be in the style of Aesop or a modern-day version, whether it should feature animals or people and how it could be made amusing. Together write and draw the fable on a large sheet of paper. Leave it on display while working on the lesson.

With the lower-achievers

With adult support

Choose from:

1 Make sure the children can remember the features of a fable. They can look at the list written on the board during the whole-class session. Look at one or two more of Aesop's fables and discuss the features of each that are typical of a fable, including its moral. Ask the children to choose their favourite fable and write it in their own words. Encourage them to choose different fables and then make a classroom edition of Aesop's Fables, which they can also illustrate.

2 Working closely with the group, choose a moral from Aesop and together draft a modern fable. Help the children to write the fable. For example, 'The Lion and the Mouse' could be retold as a tale about a boy who thought he was clever at everything in school and who used to ridicule the girl he thought was no good at

anything. But he found one day he didn't understand the science lesson and was very grateful when the girl was able to help him.

3 Give out copies of Resource sheet 7a and read the captions for the pictures with the children. Help them to make up the ending of the fable. Challenge them to write their own fable on the back of the sheet using the moral at the bottom. Give support where necessary.

4 Let the children choose one of Aesop's fables and make a play from it. Help them to practise it for a class performance. One of the children could act as narrator to tell the moral.

Teacher-independent activities

Choose from:

1 Ask the children to choose their favourite fable from Aesop. They could write their own version of the fable and illustrate it. Alternatively, as a group they could make up a version to act out. Remind them to include the moral at the end. If writing is difficult, they could record the fable in their own words onto a cassette.

2 Let the children complete Resource sheet 7a. They could work in pairs for this activity.

3 Ask the children to work in pairs to choose one of the morals from the list written during the whole-class session. They should make up a new fable to go with the moral. Remind them to include all the features of a fable.

Plenary session

- Ask children who wrote new fables to read them to the class, leaving out the moral at the end. Encourage the class to guess what the moral is.

- Ask one of the children who wrote one of Aesop's fables in their own words to share it with the class.

- Let the children who made a play from one of Aesop's fables give a class performance.

Lesson Two

Intended learning

- To revise the terms 'noun' and 'pronoun'.

- To consolidate the relationship between nouns and pronouns.

With the whole class

Before the lesson, collect an assortment of small objects and pictures of people (such as a baby, a boy, a girl, a man, a woman and several people together).

- Put the objects into a 'feely' bag and turn the pictures face down. Ask for volunteers to come and take an object from the bag or turn over a picture. They should then write the name on the board. Agree that these are nouns.

- Remind the children of the term 'pronoun' and write it on the board. Discuss what it means. Read a few sentences to them that use the nouns all the time instead of nouns and pronouns. For example, 'The hare decided that the hare would challenge the tortoise to a race,' and 'Matthew said that Matthew wanted Matthew's dinner.' Agree that these sound silly. Substitute pronouns where the children suggest they should go.

- Challenge the children to tell you the pronouns for each of the nouns written on the board. Let them come and write the pronoun beside each noun, for example beside 'man' they write 'he' and beside 'book' they write 'it'. Challenge them to name the personal pronouns that have not been used yet (I, you and we).

- Ask the children whether they can remember the possessive pronouns for each noun. Remind them of the sentence 'Matthew said that Matthew wanted Matthew's dinner.' What word did they put in place of the third 'Matthew'? Agree that this is a possessive pronoun.

- Invite volunteers to come to the board and write possessive pronouns beside the nouns and personal pronouns (his, hers, its and their/s).

■ Read a few lines from 'The Hare and the Tortoise'. Ask the children to put up their hands when they hear a noun. They could come and write the noun on the board and then write its personal pronoun and possessive pronoun. For example, 'it' is the personal pronoun to replace 'the hare' and 'its' is the possessive pronoun.

■ Play 'Noun and Pronoun Basketball'. Divide the class into two teams and name them after local areas, for example 'The Richmond Rompers' or 'The Bradford Bulls'. Using your collection of objects and pictures, ask a child to tell you either a personal or a possessive pronoun for the item you show them. If they are correct, they score a 'basket' for their team.

With the lower-achievers

With adult support

Choose from:

1 Prepare a set of cards, each with either a personal or a possessive pronoun written on it. Play a game using the cards, some tokens and your collection of objects. The cards are placed face down on the table and the children have to take one and read it. They should choose an object that fits the card. For example, if they take the card 'he', they should choose a picture of a boy or a man, or if they take the card 'it', they should choose an object. If they are correct, they win a token. The winner is the child with the highest number of tokens at the end of the game.

2 Give out copies of Resource sheet 7b. Help the children to give each noun on the top of the sheet the correct personal and possessive pronoun. (These should already be written on the board.) They should then rewrite the sentences replacing the nouns with the appropriate pronoun. Finally, they have to write sentences for some possessive pronouns.

3 Play a game of 'Quick-fire Pronouns'. Agree a set time, for example one minute. Say to different children a noun and the type of pronoun you want, for example *"Benjamin, a house's personal pronoun"* (it) or *"Lu Chun, a girl's possessive pronoun"* (her/s) How many can the children do in the set time? Be careful not to pressurise them – the game should be fun!

Teacher-independent activities

Choose from:

1 Prepare a set of cards, each with either a personal or a possessive pronoun written on it. Give the children your collection of objects, tiddlywinks and a 'Snakes and Ladders' board. They play a game where they take one of the cards, read it and then choose an object to go with it. For example, if they take the card that says 'her/s', they should choose a female picture. If the others agree they are correct, they move their tiddlywink one space along the board. When they reach the base of a ladder or a snake, they go up it (they don't go down from a snake's head). The winner is the child who gets to the top of the board first.

2 Let the children complete Resource sheet 7b in pairs for support. Read through the sheet with them before letting them work independently.

3 Have written out an extract from one of the fables with no pronouns at all – just the nouns repeated every time. Ask the children to work in pairs to cross out the nouns where necessary and replace them with personal or possessive pronouns. The text must make sense when they read it through.

Plenary session

■ Ask someone to tell you what personal and possessive pronouns are. Do all the children know when to use them?

■ Play a game of 'Quick-fire Pronouns'. Set an egg-timer going and say to different children a noun and the type of pronoun you want, for example *"Fiona – a dog's possessive pronoun"* (its) or *"Pritpal, a man's personal pronoun."* (he) How many can they do before the sand runs through? Challenge them to beat their own record.

Lesson Three

Intended learning

■ To understand and use correctly the term 'antonym'.

■ To investigate antonyms.

With the whole class

Before the lesson, write on the board 'shut', 'white', 'large', 'over', 'happy' and 'tall'.

■ Tell the children you are going to say pairs of words and they should try to work out what they are. Slowly say pairs of opposites such as 'dark and light', 'laugh and cry', 'throw and 'catch and so on. What do the children think the words have in common? Agree they are opposites and write the word on the board. Tell them that there is another word for 'opposites' – 'antonyms'. Write it beside 'opposites'. Read the word with the children helping them to pronounce and spell it correctly.

■ Point to the words you wrote before the lesson and ask the children to read them. Ask for volunteers to tell you what the antonyms are. Let them come and write the antonyms beside each word ('open', 'black', 'small', 'under', 'sad' and 'short').

■ Ask the children to suggest other pairs of antonyms. Let them come and write them on the board. Explain that antonyms can be used for verbs, nouns and adjectives, for example 'cry'/'laugh' or 'throw'/'catch' (verbs), 'child'/'adult' or 'floor'/'ceiling' (noun) and 'empty'/'full' or 'heavy'/'light' (adjectives). Encourage the children to think of more examples. Let them add these to the list.

■ Relate antonyms to the fables you have been reading with the class. For example, the hare is fast and the tortoise is slow.

With the lower-achievers

With adult support

Choose from:

1 Make sure the children can recognise and read the word 'antonym' and that they understand what it means. Find some more words and their opposites. Help them to make an 'Antonym Chart', listing as many pairs of antonyms as they can think of or find. Challenge them to find words that have more than one antonym, for example 'light' has 'dark' or 'heavy'.

2 Look through a favourite fable from *Aesop's Fables* for examples of words that have antonyms. Help the children to make a word wall with each set of antonyms in the 'bricks'.

3 Give the children copies of Resource sheet 7c. Help them to find the correct antonyms from the words in the table. They should then make the word circle, turn it to align the antonyms and write them in a list.

Teacher-independent activities

Choose from:

1 Give the children a well-known rhyme or short story and ask them to have fun finding as many antonyms for the words as they can. For example, 'Big Jack Horner stood in the middle'.

2 Give the children copies of Resource sheet 7c to complete in pairs.

Plenary session

■ Play an antonym game where you call out a word and the children have to shout out the opposite. You may prefer to ask them to whisper the opposites!

■ Play the same game but choose children to be the quizmasters instead of you.

■ Look at this modern-day fable. Read the moral and then make up your own ending.

Moral: everybody is good at something.

Sam found reading and maths hard.

Every day he played football in the yard.

The teacher chose the team for a match. Sam was the reserve.

On the day of the match the goalkeeper was ill.

'You'll have to be goalie, Sam,' said the teacher. 'Do your best.'

■ Write the caption that goes with your picture at the end of the story.

_____

■ On the back of this sheet write and draw a fable to show this moral.

If you try hard enough, you will succeed.

■ Read these nouns and then write a personal pronoun and a possessive pronoun for each one. One has been done for you.

hare

boy

woman

__it__ __its__   _____ _____   _____ _____

■ Rewrite these sentences using the correct personal pronouns for the nouns that are underlined. One has been done for you.

The children went out to play.   _They_____

The house was burned down.   _____

The man set off to work.   _____

The queen was crowned in June.   _____

■ Write a sentence for these possessive pronouns.

yours   its   theirs   our

_____

_____

_____

_____

■ Draw a circle around the antonym for each word in the left-hand column. One has been done for you.

shut	closed	(open)	lock
white	yellow	blue	black
hill	mountain	valley	river
large	small	big	huge
over	through	under	above
happy	joyful	sad	pleased
floor	room	door	ceiling
tall	high	big	short
empty	bare	full	vacant

■ Make the word circle and find the antonyms. Write them on a piece of paper.

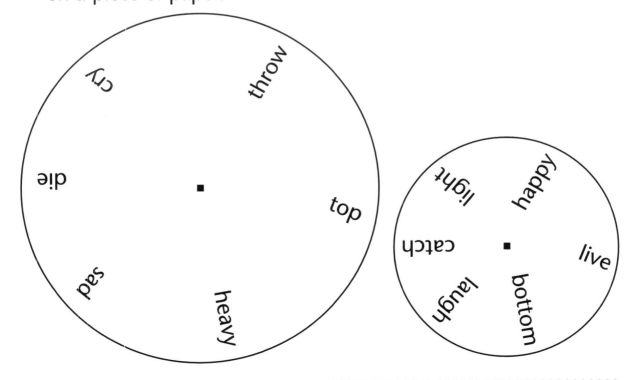

Traditional stories

Overall aims

- To revisit some well-known traditional stories.
- To identify the common features of traditional stories.
- To explore ambiguities that may arise from sentence contractions.
- To explore onomatopoeia.

Featured book

Grimms Fairy Tales translated by Peter Carter, Oxford University Press, 1997, or any chosen collection of fairytales

Lesson One
. . . .

Intended learning

- To revisit some well-known traditional stories.
- To identify the common features of traditional stories.

With the whole class

- Write the titles of two or three well-known traditional stories on the board, such as 'Goldilocks', 'Dick Whittington' and 'Jack and the Beanstalk'. Ask the children for two ways of describing this group of stories (fairytales/stories or traditional tales/stories).

- Invite the children to give you the names of other traditional tales. Let them write these on the board themselves, but give help with spelling if it is needed. When and where do the children usually listen to or read traditional tales? Which are their favourites? Why? Which is their least favourite? Why?

- Tell the children that most fairytales are very old and have been passed down orally. Do they know what this means? Explain that the oral history of traditional tales accounts for slight variations in the detail of some stories, but the basic plots remain the same. Ask the children to suggest why traditional tales were told in the first place. (To put over a message such as hope being always present; to convey a moral such as 'good triumphs over evil'; to explain or illustrate a true event such as the rags-to-riches story of Dick Whittington.)

- Tell the children they are going to explore some traditional tales in order to discover the similarities between them. Together, look at the contents page of *Grimms Fairy Tales* and choose at least three stories to read. Explain that while they are enjoying the stories, they should try to notice what similarities there are between them.

- When you have read the tales, discuss together what the children noticed. They may suggest things such as: there is usually a young, beautiful heroine and a young, handsome hero; there is one character (usually ugly) who represents evil; there is an 'opposing' character who represents good; evil is always overpowered by good; there is often a transformation from poverty to riches; there is usually a happy ending for the 'good' characters and the 'bad' ones get their just deserts.

- On the board, list the agreed points and leave them up while working on this lesson. Encourage the children to come and write next to each point an example from one of the stories explored, for example beside 'young and beautiful heroine' one child might write 'Snow White' and another may put 'Cinderella'. Ask the children to name other traditional stories (not read in this lesson) that fit most of the categories.

With the lower-achievers

With adult support

Choose from:

1   Look at the list of the characteristics of traditional tales that was written on the board during the whole-class session. Make sure the children understand each point. Discuss them together and choose which tales make good examples of each point. Tell the children that most tales will fit most of the items on the list. Help the children to make their own chart of the features of traditional tales and fill in the sections with examples.

2   Give the children copies of Resource sheet 8a. Help the children to decide which characters from traditional tales fit into the categories in the table.

3   Together, choose one of the tales from the featured book and work with the children to retell it with a modern-day setting. Help them to practise a role-play to give a class performance. They could also write modern versions of several tales and make a class book.

Teacher-independent activities

Choose from:

1   Let the children work in pairs to complete Resource sheet 8a.

2   Give the children copies of Generic sheet 1 (page 118) and the chart on the top half of Resource sheet 8a. Ask them to complete the chart in relation to the characters in the story of 'Sleeping Beauty'. Do all the categories apply?

3   Let the children choose one of the tales from *Grimms Fairy Tales* and read it together.

Plenary session

■   Invite the children who practised role-playing one of the tales to give a class performance. Challenge the others to identify the various characteristics of a traditional tale from the performance.

■   Ask the children who wrote modern-day versions of traditional tales to read their stories to the others. Did they remember to include the characteristics explored in the lesson?

■   Ask the children who worked with the story of 'Sleeping Beauty' to tell the others how the characters in the story fit into the accepted features of traditional tales.

Lesson Two

Intended learning

■   To understand and use correctly the term 'ambiguous'.

■   To explore ambiguities that may arise from sentence contractions.

With the whole class

■   Write on the board 'point', 'fire' and 'light'. Explain that these words can have more than one meaning. For example, 'The boosters wouldn't fire so the rocket didn't move,' or 'The boss had to fire the lazy worker.' Can the children give you two meanings for the other words? Ask them how they know which meaning is being used in a piece of writing where there is more than one possible meaning. They should say how they know which meaning makes sense. Explain that the context of a word is very important for making its meaning clear.

■   Write 'ambiguous' on the board and read it with the children. Does anybody know what it means? Explain that we use the term for unclear meanings or double meanings. Read the following statement (from the *NLS* document): 'Police shot man with knife.' Ask for a volunteer to tell you why this is ambiguous. Could they use a knife to shoot someone? Which interpretation is the only sensible one?

■   Read 'Nothing acts faster than Anadin' and 'Baby changing room' (from the *NLS* document). Again, explore the ambiguities in each example.

■   Discuss some statements that are ambiguous, using the traditional tales as a basis, for example 'Cinderella went to the ball in glass slippers.' How is this ambiguous?

■   Encourage the children to think of other words that could be ambiguous ('strike', 'mummy', 'case', 'long'). Let them write their words on the board and leave them up. Challenge them to make an ambiguous statement with some of the words, for example 'Men strike at airport.' Ask the children whether they think this means that the men stopped work or they hit the airport with something.

- Where might the children find these short statements? Look at several newspaper headlines and point out that they are contracted sentences. They put across the main points of the story in a shortened version. Discuss the headlines. What do they mean? What would the full sentence be? Do they make sense in the contracted form? Ask the children to look out for examples of ambiguous headlines and bring them to school to share.

With the lower-achievers

With adult support
Choose from:

1   Make sure the children understand the meaning of 'ambiguous'. Look for more examples of words with double meanings and discuss them together. Help them to write a sentence for each meaning of the words. Challenge them to find words with more than two meanings. They could use a dictionary for this.

2   Look again at the ambiguous headlines from the whole-class session. Discuss them together making sure the children see the nonsense interpretation of each. Work with them to think of and write more examples that are ambiguous, for example 'Paying car park' or 'Disabled toilet'.

3   Give out copies of Resource sheet 8b. Help the children to match each word to a meaning and then find a second meaning. Encourage them to use dictionaries. Ask the children to tell you how the sentences are ambiguous. Discuss them together. Help them to write the sentences in a way that makes the meaning clear.

Teacher-independent activities
Choose from:

1   Give the children at least five words with more than one meaning, such as 'pass', 'post', 'bat', 'blow' and 'close'. Ask them to look in the dictionary to find as many meanings as they can for these words. Ask them to make a list of the

words and write their meanings. If writing is difficult, they could record their words and sentences on a cassette.

2   Give the children copies of Resource sheet 8b to complete in pairs. Read it through with them before letting them work independently.

3   Ask the children to work in pairs and use the ambiguous statements discussed in the whole-class session to write a nonsense story that makes the headline correct, for example the police did indeed shoot a man using a knife or a lady changed her baby for another in the baby changing room!

Plenary session

- Did the children enjoy this lesson? Ask for a volunteer to tell you what 'ambiguous' means. What strategies do we use to understand an intended meaning?

- Play a game where you write on the board a word that has two meanings and the children work in pairs to check the meanings in a dictionary and put up their hands to tell you what they have found.

Lesson Three

Intended learning

- To explore onomatopoeia.
- To use onomatopoeia in own work.

With the whole class

Before this lesson, collect some comics for the children to look at.

- Look at some of the comics together and let the children point out the words that are 'sound words', for example 'splat', 'Gggrrrrrr', 'THWACK', 'purr'. List them on the board. Why do the children think these words are used in the comics?

- Explain that when we use words that are written as the sound they try to convey, we call this onomatopoeia. Write 'onomatopoeia' on the board and spend a few moments reading it and looking at the phonemes together. Tell the children that onomatopoeic words don't have to be new or invented. For example, 'miaow' and 'sizzle' are both examples of 'real' words that are onomatopoeic. Challenge the children to think of other onomatopoeic words. Let them come and write the words on the board.

■ Together, make up or choose some onomatopoeic words for a pin dropping onto the floor, somebody falling into a very muddy puddle and an alligator having a bath in the river. Write these new words on the board.

■ Look at some of the traditional tales from the featured book. How would some of the incidents here be recorded if they were in comic form? For example, when the mirror tells the Wicked Queen she is not the fairest in the land, what is her reaction? ('Grrrrrrrr!' or 'Aaaaaahhhhhhhh!') Or when the Fairy Godmother first appears to Cinderella, how does she arrive? ('Whuusshhh') Write their words on the board.

With the lower-achievers

With adult support

Choose from:

1 Make sure the children understand what 'onomatopoeia' means. If necessary, go over the teaching points again. Look through the comics and the featured book together for more onomatopoeic words. Help the children to make a large poster showing onomatopoeic words and encourage them to add to this as they find more examples. Let them illustrate the words on the poster.

2 Make a set of onomatopoeic word cards using words such as 'sizzle', 'whoosh', 'crunch', 'zap', 'miaow', 'crackle', 'splat', 'moo', 'gurgle', 'snap', 'grrrr' and 'plop'. Place the cards in a pile on the table face down. The children take a card, read the onomatopoeic word and then suggest where it might be used. For example, if they read 'plop' they may suggest a drop of water falling into a bowl of water. Help them to write their sentences using the words.

3 Give out copies of Resource sheet 8c. Ask the children to read the onomatopoeic words and write them in some sentences. Challenge them to make up some of their own words.

4 Work closely together to help the children to make up new words for situations such as a large window smashing, a waterfall, screwing up paper and so on. Let them write their new words as graphically as possible, using shape and colour to express the meaning.

Teacher-independent activities

Choose from:

1 Let the children complete Resource sheet 8c in pairs for support. Read it through with them first.

2 Let the children choose one of the traditional stories from the featured book and practise a role-play. They should use onomatopoeic words at relevant points in the story. They could make up their own words or use 'real' onomatopoeia.

3 Give the children copies of Generic sheet 1 (page 118). Ask them to work in pairs to devise or find onomatopoeic words for some of the frames in the story, such as 'The good fairy waved her wand with a woosh,' and 'the princess fell to the floor with a craaaassshh.'

Plenary session

■ As a class, make up some onomatopoeic poems, such as:

> Crackle went the fire
> 'Snooooorrrrr' said Dad.

> Splat went the rain
> Squish said my welly-boots.

Remind the children that poems do not have to rhyme.

■ Look at this chart. It has in it features of traditional tales.

Good	Bad	Beautiful/ handsome	Ugly	Becomes rich	Lives happily ever after

■ Write the names of these characters in the correct columns in the chart. They may go in more than one column

- ❖ Sleeping Beauty
- ❖ Little Red Riding Hood
- ❖ The Ugly Sisters
- ❖ Prince Charming
- ❖ Cinderella
- ❖ The Giant
- ❖ The Wolf
- ❖ The Wicked Stepmother
- ❖ Jack
- ❖ The Beast
- ❖ Beauty

■ Now write the names of some other characters in the chart.

■ Answer these questions.

How were traditional tales first told? _____

_____

Why were traditional tales first told? _____

_____

orally	message	moral	word of mouth

■ Write a short tale on the back of this sheet using some of the ideas in traditional stories.

■ Match each word to a meaning and then write another meaning. Use a dictionary to help you.

A child's name for their mother.	coach _____
The noise when a bell is pulled.	fire _____
Somebody who trains a team to play well.	point _____
To sack someone from their job.	mummy _____
The sharp end of something.	ring _____

■ What do you think the following sentences really mean? Circle the sentences that make sense.

When he saw the flower, the man with the big nose picked it.

When the man with the big nose saw the flower he picked it.

When the man with the big nose saw the flower he picked his nose.

Cinderella went to the ball in glass slippers.

Cinderella travelled to the ball inside glass slippers.

Cinderella wore glass slippers to the ball.

■ Write some more ambiguous sentences.

■ Find the definition of 'onomatopoeia' in a dictionary. Write it here.

_____

_____

■ Read these onomatopoeic words.

| sizzle | woof | crunch | slurp | pop |
| cuckoo | purr | squelch | crack | moo |

■ Choose five of them and write a sentence for each one. For example, 'The balloon burst with a loud pop.'

_____

_____

_____

_____

_____

■ Make up your own onomatopoeic words for the following.

the giant falling off the beanstalk _____

Cinderella's carriage wheels _____

Baby Bear crying _____

water running out of a bath _____

snowflakes falling _____

disco music _____

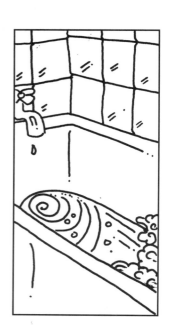

Narrative poems

Overall aims

- To use the chosen poem as a basis for understanding the term 'narrative'.
- To explore a range of narrative poems.
- To use the poetry as a stimulus for own work.

Featured book

The Puffin Book of Utterly Brilliant Poetry edited by Brian Patten, Puffin Books, 1998

Lesson One

Chosen poem

'Greedyguts' by Kit Wright, page 68

Intended learning

- To use the chosen poem as a basis for understanding the term 'narrative'.
- To use the chosen poem as a stimulus for own work.

With the whole class

- Enlarge a copy of 'Greedyguts' and have a dictionary ready. Tell the children that this poem is by Kit Wright and it is a narrative poem. Write 'narrative' on the board. Ask the children what it means. Do they know a word that is similar such as 'narrate' or 'narrator'? Ask them to tell you what these mean.

- Invite a volunteer to come and look in the dictionary for 'narrative'. Ask them to give you a synonym such as 'story'. Encourage the children to guess from this what a narrative poem might be. Explain that narrative poems are stories in poetical form.

- Read 'Greedyguts' to the children, letting them follow the text. (If possible, use the original anthology so that the children can see the illustrations.) Ask them to retell the story in the poem. How does the story move from its opening to its conclusion? Could the poem have a follow-up? Encourage the children to

suggest what might happen next. Agree one or two alternative ideas and write them on the board, for example 'Greedyguts started to cry,' or 'The narrator finished Greedyguts's food.'

- Discuss the difference between a narrative poem and narrative prose. Explain that prose is 'ordinary' writing – non-poetical. Agree that there is no rhyme, rhythm or verse structure to narrative prose and narrative poetry is likely to have fewer descriptive passages and use fewer words.

- Challenge the children to think of other rhymes or poems that are narrative poems, for example 'Who Started It?' (Michael Rosen) or 'Gruesome' (Roger McGough). Do they think narrative poems are interesting? Why/why not?

With the lower-achievers

With adult support

Choose from:

1   Read the poem again with the children letting them join in where they can. Ask them to retell the story. Make sure they give the right sequence of events. Are there any words or phrases that they have difficulty with, such as 'vaster' or 'To even the score'? Explain what they mean or use a dictionary to look for the words together. Help the children to recite the chorus of the poem. Encourage them to use intonation and volume to express the meaning.

2   Give out copies of Resource sheet 9a. The children should decide which of the traditional rhymes are narrative poems. Tell them to ask themselves the question, 'Does it tell a story?' The answers are then to be found in the wordsearch, but the titles of the rhymes have been split up.

3   Look through other anthologies (or the poetry chapters in this series of books) for narrative poems. Explore these together. Compare the subject matter and the style of narrative (1st person or 3rd person, rhyming or non-rhyming, verse patterns, rhythm and so on) with those of 'Greedyguts'. Help the children to choose one or two favourites to share during the plenary session. Encourage them to say why they like the poems they have chosen.

4   Using Resource sheet 9b, the children cut out the pictures from the story, including the blank frame. They then put the pictures in the correct sequence and in the final blank picture frame draw the actual ending or an alternative one.

Teacher-independent activities

Choose from:

1   Let the children complete Resource sheet 9a in pairs for support. You may need to explain to them what the task is.

2   Ask the children to work in pairs. Give them an anthology of poetry at a suitable reading level and ask them to decide which poems are narratives. Challenge them to write the story of one poem in their own words.

3   Give the children copies of Resource sheet 9b to complete. When they have drawn a picture in the blank box they could arrange the pictures around a copy of the poem with lines drawn to the parts of the poem that the pictures match.

Plenary session

■   Ask the children who explored other narrative poems to share their favourites with the class. They could read the poems themselves or if this is too difficult you could read them. Encourage them to explain why they like the poems.

■   Read 'Greedyguts' again, letting the children who practised reciting the chorus say that part of the poem at the right time.

■   Does everybody know what narrative poetry is? Ask for examples other than 'Greedyguts'.

Lesson Two

Intended learning

■   To explore a range of narrative poems by other poets.

■   To use the poetry as a stimulus for own work.

With the whole class

■   Ask the children to remind you what 'narrative' means. Ask them to tell you the word for 'ordinary' writing (prose). If necessary, remind them.

■   Look through the anthology with the children and explore other narrative poems, such as 'Chocolate Cake' (Michael Rosen), 'Silly Old Baboon' (Spike Milligan) or 'Once Upon a Time' (John Agard). You could use other anthologies and poems here if you prefer.

■   Discuss each poem explored. Ask different children to retell the story in their own words. Encourage them to say whether they think the rhyming (or non-rhyming) pattern, the rhythm, the verse structure, the choice of words and the use of alliteration or onomatopoeia help in the poem's narrative. Ask them to give reasons for their answers.

■   Discuss together some personal experiences that would be good ideas for narrative poetry, for example a visit by a dreaded person, an embarrassing moment in the doctor's surgery or coming in filthy from playing outside. List the ideas. Write a short narrative poem together, perhaps on a day in somebody's life. For example,

> At 7 o'clock my mum got up
> At 8 o'clock she put on her make-up
> At 9 o'clock she walked out of the door
> At 10 o'clock she left our shores
> At 11 o'clock she arrived in France

and so on.

Remind the children that the poem doesn't have to rhyme. Write it on a large sheet of paper and leave it displayed while working on this lesson.

With the lower-achievers

With adult support

Choose from:

1   Let the children choose one of the poems explored in the whole-class session and work with them to role-play the story, making sure parts of the poem are recited during the play. (This may need to be done away from the main classroom.)

2   Look at the list of ideas for narrative poetry that was written during the whole-class session. Challenge the children to think of some others, such as getting lost in a shop, meeting a fierce-looking dog, amusing incidents with baby siblings and so on. Agree a favourite and help them to write a narrative poem. Remind them it doesn't have to rhyme.

3   Help the children to complete the narrative poem on Resource sheet 9c.

Teacher-independent activities

Choose from:

1   Ask the children to work in pairs. Give them an anthology of poetry at a suitable reading level. They should decide together which are narrative poems and then choose one. They should either write or record on a cassette the story told by the poem.

2   Give the children copies of Resource sheet 9c to complete in pairs.

Plenary session

■   Let the children who did a role-play of a poem give a class performance. Did they remember to include some quotations from the poem?

■   Ask for volunteers from those who wrote their own poems to read these to the class.

■   Do the children like narrative poetry? Encourage them to give reasons for their answers. Which is their favourite narrative poem? Who is their favourite poet? Why?

Greedyguts
by Kit Wright

I sat in the cafe and sipped at a Coke.
There sat down beside me a WHOPPING great bloke
Who sighed as he elbowed me into the wall:
'Your trouble, my boy, is your belly's too small!
Your bottom's too thin! Take a lesson from me:
I may not be nice, but I'm GREAT, you'll agree,
And I've lasted a lifetime by playing this hunch:
The bigger the breakfast, the larger the lunch!

The larger the lunch, the huger the supper.
The deeper the teapot, the vaster the cupper.
The fatter the sausage, the fuller the tea.
The MORE on the table, the BETTER for me!'

His elbows moved in and his elbows moved out;
His belly grew bigger, chins wobbled about,
As forkful by forkful and plate after plate,
He ate and he ate and he ate and he ATE!

I hardly could breathe, I was squashed out of shape,
So under the table I made my escape.

'Aha!' he rejoiced, 'when it's put to the test,
The fellow who's fattest will come off the best!
Remember, my boy, when it comes to the crunch:
The bigger the breakfast, the larger the lunch!

The larger the lunch, the huger the supper.
The deeper the teapot, the vaster the cupper.
The fatter the sausage, the fuller the tea.
The MORE on the table, the BETTER for me!'

A lady came by who was scrubbing the floor
With a mop and a bucket. To even the score,
I lifted that bucket of water and said,
As I poured the whole lot of it over his head:

'I've found all my life, it's a pretty sure bet:
The FULLER the bucket, the WETTER you GET!'

■ Tick (✔) the rhymes that are narrative poems.
(Ask yourself, 'Does it tell a story?')

Humpty Dumpty ☐   Mary, Mary ☐
Jack and Jill ☐   Three blind mice ☐
Little Miss Muffet ☐   Baa, baa, black sheep ☐

■ You will find the answers in this wordsearch. Be careful because the words have been split up!

H	U	T	H	R	E	E	A	N	M
U	E	T	M	Y	A	J	D	T	U
M	L	P	U	T	B	L	N	I	F
P	T	M	F	P	M	I	A	L	F
T	T	U	F	M	K	C	A	J	E
Y	I	H	E	U	T	H	R	I	T
B	L	I	N	D	S	S	J	L	N
M	I	C	E	S	S	I	M	L	A

THREE →
LITTLE ↑
MUFFET ↓
JACK ←
BLIND →
DUMPTY ↑
JILL ↓
MISS ←
MICE →
AND ↑
HUMPTY ↓

■ Write the titles of two more narrative rhymes.

_____

_____

■ Think about what you do in a day. Write a narrative poem about your day. Your poem does not have to rhyme.

At 8 o'clock I _____

At 10 o'clock I _____

At 12 o'clock I _____

At 2 o'clock I _____

At 4 o'clock I _____

At 6 o'clock I _____

■ Illustrate some of the things in your poem.

Poems to aid poetry writing

Overall aims

- To understand rhyming patterns in 'a, b, c' terms.

- To explore the structure of the chosen poems.

- To use the chosen poetry as a stimulus for adding own verses or substituting own ideas.

Featured books

A Child's Garden of Verses by Robert Louis Stevenson, (any chosen edition)

A First Poetry Book compiled by John Foster, Oxford University Press, 1979 (1989 edition)

Lesson One

Chosen poems

'From a Railway Carriage' and 'At the Seaside' by Robert Louis Stevenson, page 75

'Sweet Song' by Vernon Scannell, page 76

Intended learning

- To understand and identify rhyming patterns in terms of 'a, b, c'.

- To explore the structure of the chosen poems.

- To use the chosen poetry as a stimulus for adding own verses.

With the whole class

- Enlarge copies of 'From a Railway Carriage', 'At the Seaside' and 'Sweet Song'.

- Share 'From a Railway Carriage', letting the children follow the text. Can they say what the poem is about? Explain that the rhythm of the poem represents the rhythm of the train as it speeds through the countryside. Ask them to identify the words that rhyme. Ask different children to show you different rhyme families. Tell the children that sometimes a poem's rhyming pattern is described by giving each family of rhyming words a letter, 'a', 'b', 'c' and so on. In 'From a Railway Carriage', the

rhyming pattern is a, a, b, b, c, c, d, d. In the first verse these words are 'witches' and 'ditches' (a, a), 'battle' and 'cattle' (b, b), 'plain' and 'rain' (c, c) and 'eye' and 'by' (d, d). Ask volunteers to point out the words of the equivalent a,b,c,d patterns in verse two.

- Discuss together the structure of the poem. Explore how many verses there are, how many lines in each verse and whether the poem has regular or irregular rhyme and rhythm patterns. Do they think this poem could have been written today? Encourage them to tell you why they think this.

- Share 'At the Seaside' and ask some of the children to point out the rhyming words. Can they tell you these in 'a, b, c' terms? (a, a, b; c, c, b – 'sea', 'me', 'shore' and 'cup', 'up', 'more') If the children are a little unsure, use some other poems from the anthology to explain and give more practice. What can they tell you about the structure of 'At the Seaside'? Remind them of the ideas you discussed together about the structure of 'From a Railway Carriage'.

- Read 'Sweet Song' to the children, letting them follow the text. Ask for volunteers to point out the rhyming words in the first verse. Challenge the children to identify the rhyming pattern in 'a, b, c' terms (a, b, c, b). Is the rhyme pattern regular? Is this the pattern through the whole poem?

- Explore the structure of 'Sweet Song'. Ask the children to tell you how many verses there are. How many lines are there in each verse? Is there a rhythm pattern? Is it regular?

- Together think of other sweets that could be added to the poem. Using its structure and style as a model, together write a verse to add to the poem. Leave a list of sweets and the poem on the board while working on this lesson.

With the lower-achievers

With adult support

Choose from:

1   Make sure the children understand how the 'a, b, c' format is applied to the rhyming words of a poem. Using the enlarged copies of each chosen poem, ask the children to circle the sets of

rhyming words with different colours. Ask them to write 'a', 'b', 'c' or 'd' beside the sets of rhyming words. Together, explore some other poems in *A Child's Garden of Verses* and discuss their rhyming patterns using the 'a, b, c' format.

2   Using copies of Resource sheet 10a, help the children to work out the rhyming patterns of the poems and write 'a', 'b' and 'c' in the appropriate boxes. Give reading support if necessary. They should find another poem to write on the back of the sheet and put the 'a, b, c' rhyming pattern at the ends of the lines.

3   Give the children copies of Resource sheet 10b. Help them to write a second verse to the poem. They could use the words on the sheet or make up their own. Challenge them to write a third verse on the back of the sheet. Give support if necessary.

Teacher-independent activities

Choose from:

1   Give the children copies of Resource sheet 10a to complete. You might wish to let them work in pairs for support with the reading.

2   Ask the children to work in pairs to choose some sweets from the list drawn up during the whole-class session. They should write another verse for the poem. If keeping to the style and structure is difficult, let them create their verse freely.

Plenary session

■   Ask for volunteers from those who explored the rhyming patterns of other poems to tell the class what they discovered. Were they able to identify the 'a, b, c' format of their chosen poems?

■   Let the children who wrote their own poems or extra verses read them to the class.

■   Does everybody understand the 'a, b, c' format for rhyming patterns? Is there anything difficult about it that needs to be explained a little more?

Lesson Two

Chosen poems

'The Quarrel' by Eleanor Farjeon, page 77

Intended learning

■   To explore the structure of the chosen poem.

■   To use the chosen poetry as a stimulus for substituting own ideas.

With the whole class

■   Enlarge a copy of 'The Quarrel'. Remind the children of the work they did on rhyming, structure and verse patterns in Lesson One. Tell them that now they are going to read a poem with a different structure of both verse and rhyme. Ask them to try to think about these while you are reading the poem.

■   Read 'The Quarrel' to the children, letting them follow the text. What is the poem about? Do they understand how the child in the poem is feeling? Ask the children if they think the poet has captured the idea of what it's like to quarrel with a sibling or a friend. Explain that the lines 'Then suddenly my brother/Thumped me on the back' mean that he gave a friendly thump.

■   Invite the children to tell you about the structure of the poem. (There are two verses of eight lines each, it has a regular rhyming pattern of a, b, a, b, c, d, c, d, and its rhythm pattern is regular with three beats in every line.)

■   Discuss together some other aspects of sibling or friend relationships that could be used to write poetry, such as times when they help each other, a younger sibling's feelings about hand-me-downs or what they compete about. List the ideas. Agree on one and together write a short poem. Remind the children it doesn't have to rhyme. Write the poem on a large sheet of paper and leave it displayed while working on this lesson.

With the lower-achievers

With adult support

Choose from:

1 Read 'The Quarrel' again together, encouraging the children to join in. Discuss what it is like to quarrel with a sibling or a friend. Work closely with the children and help them to write a group poem about a quarrel.

2 Give out copies of Resource sheet 10c. Help the children to read the poem and discuss the rhyming pattern, the 'a, b, c' format and the rhythm pattern. Challenge them to make up a second verse to the poem. They could use the words on the sheet or make up their own.

3 Help the children to learn 'The Quarrel' and make a play about it. They should practise reciting the poem and acting the play for a performance during the plenary session.

Teacher-independent activities

Choose from:

1 Give the children copies of Resource sheet 10c to complete.

2 Ask the children to work in pairs. They should choose an idea from the list written during the whole-class session and together write a poem. Remind them it doesn't have to rhyme or be very long.

3 Let the children work in pairs and look through an anthology at a suitable reading level. Ask them to choose their favourite poem and try to learn it, or part of it, to recite to the others.

Plenary session

■ Ask somebody from the group that wrote a poem about a quarrel to read it to the class. If anybody else wrote a poem, let them share it with the others.

■ Let the group who learned 'The Quarrel' recite it and act their role-play.

■ Ask the children who chose and learned a poem to recite it to the class. Can they say why they chose their poems?

From a Railway Carriage

Faster than fairies, faster than witches,
Bridges and houses, hedges and ditches;
And charging along like troops in a battle,
All through the meadows the horses and cattle:
All of the sights of the hill and the plain
Fly as thick as driving rain;
And ever again, in the wink of an eye,
Painted stations whistle by.

Here is a child who clambers and scrambles,
All by himself and gathering brambles;
Here is a tramp who stands and gazes;
And there is the green for stringing the daisies!
Here is a cart run away in the road
Lumping along with man and load;
And here is a mill and there is a river:
Each a glimpse and gone for ever!

Robert Louis Stevenson

At the Seaside

When I was down beside the sea
A wooden spade they gave to me
To dig the sandy shore.
My holes were empty like a cup,
In every hole the sea came up,
Till it could come no more.

Robert Louis Stevenson

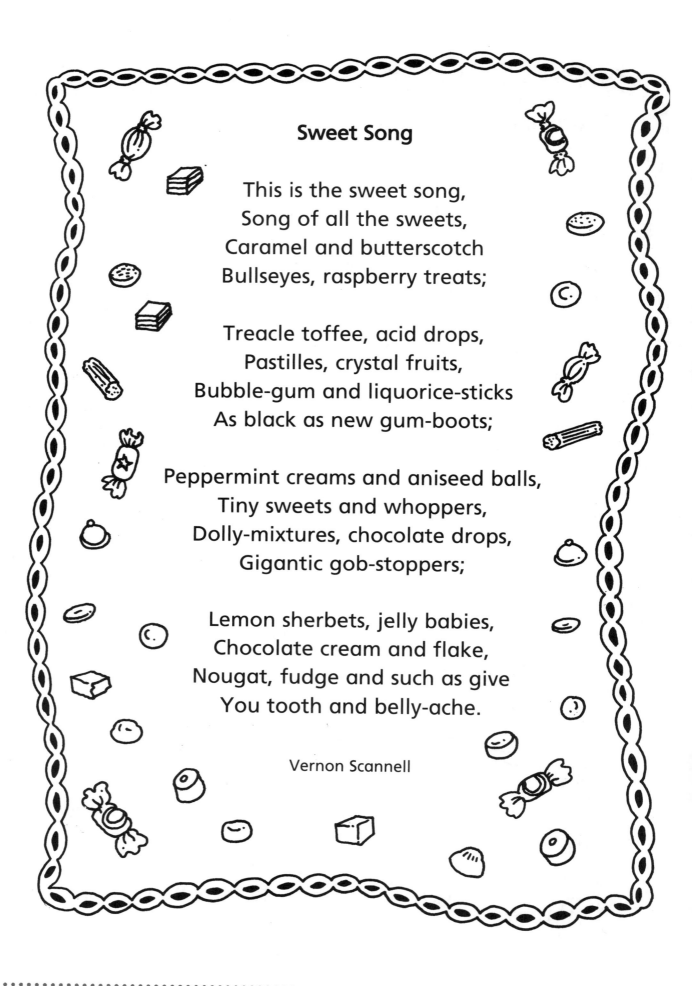

Sweet Song

This is the sweet song,
Song of all the sweets,
Caramel and butterscotch
Bullseyes, raspberry treats;

Treacle toffee, acid drops,
Pastilles, crystal fruits,
Bubble-gum and liquorice-sticks
As black as new gum-boots;

Peppermint creams and aniseed balls,
Tiny sweets and whoppers,
Dolly-mixtures, chocolate drops,
Gigantic gob-stoppers;

Lemon sherbets, jelly babies,
Chocolate cream and flake,
Nougat, fudge and such as give
You tooth and belly-ache.

Vernon Scannell

The Quarrel

I quarrelled with my brother,
I don't know what about,
One thing led to another
And somehow we fell out.
The start of it was slight,
The end of it was strong,
He said he was right,
I knew he was wrong!

We hated one another.
The afternoon turned black.
Then suddenly my brother
Thumped me on the back,
And said, 'Oh come along!
We can't go on all night -
I was in the wrong.'
So he was in the right.

Eleanor Farjeon

Name _____

■ Look at the rhyming pattern in these rhymes. Write a, b, c and so on in the box at the end of each line, like this:

Jack Spratt could eat no fat, `a`
His wife could eat no lean, `b`
And so, between them both, `c`
They licked the platter clean. `b`

One, two, three, four, ☐
Mary at the cottage door, ☐
Five, six, seven, eight, ☐
Eating cherries off a plate. ☐

I'll sing you a song, ☐
Though not very long, ☐
Yet I think it's as pretty as any, ☐
Put your hand in your purse, ☐
You'll never do worse, ☐
And give the poor singer a penny. ☐

The man in the wilderness asked of me ☐
How many strawberries grew in the sea. ☐
I answered him as I thought good, ☐
As many red herrings grew in the wood. ☐

■ Find another poem. Write it on the back of this sheet and put `a` `b` `c` at the end of the lines.

■ Read this poem.

Rainy Day IT

What can you do on a wet, rainy day?
Log on the website – get ready to play!
Monsters and villains chase through winding alleys,
Tunnels and mountains, caverns and valleys.
They'll get me, I know, if I don't run away.
"This game is finished. Are you ready to play?"
But wait just a moment – the rain is no more.
The sun has come out now. I think I'll just 'store'.

■ What is the rhyming pattern? Write the letters a, b, c and so on at the end of each line.

■ Now finish this poem about a computer game. Give the poem a rhyming pattern. You can use the words provided to help you or choose your own.

Log on to the game of 'Eternal Night'
It's _____
You'll be zapped by creatures who come out of the dark
Or _____
The virtual nightmare_____
So _____

fright	appear	right	place	park

space	away	fear	mark

■ Read this poem and then answer the questions.

Two thin ladies went out one day.
The wind came up and blew them away.
When they landed they looked such a terrible sight
The wind died down 'cos it got such a fright.

■ What are the rhyming words?

_____ and _____

_____ and _____

■ What is the rhyme format? ☐ ☐ ☐ ☐

■ What is the rhythm pattern? _____ in each line.

■ Write another verse of the poem here. Use the words below to help you.

Two fat monkeys were walking along.

They met a _____ song.

The _____ away

So _____ day.

| rain | wind | wild | snow | blew | very | wandered |

Stories from other cultures

Overall aims

- To explore stories from other cultures and discuss how they compare with own experiences.

- To understand and use correctly the term 'preposition'.

- To understand how a word can be transformed to mean its opposite by the addition of a prefix.

Featured book

The Chilli Challenge and other stories by Narinder Dhami, Angela Barry and Judith O'Neill, Heinemann, 1998

Book synopsis

The book comprises three short stories, one from the Punjab, one from Africa and one from Australia. 'The Chilli Challenge' tells of Sonny's holiday which starts badly but ends with Sonny making some new friends and being able to play his beloved cricket. In 'Nomsa and the Baboons', Nomsa is able to save her village's precious mielie crop from greedy baboons by plucking up courage to ask for help from the wise but frightening Sangoma. In 'A Strange Meeting', Jack's school trip to the Murray River leaves him wondering whether he has seen a ghost, after he meets a man who claims to be an explorer who lived in the early nineteenth century.

Lesson One

Intended learning

- To use the chosen texts to find out about the ways of life in other cultures.

- To discuss how they compare with own experiences.

With the whole class

This lesson may take more than one session.

- Show *The Chilli Challenge and other stories* to the children and tell them there are three stories in it from totally different countries. Read the story titles. Tell the children the stories are set in different places; one in the Punjab, one in Africa and the final one in Australia.

- Look at 'Nomsa and the Baboons' first. Tell the children this is the story set in southern Africa and together find the region in an atlas or on a globe. Read the story, letting the children see the illustrations.

- At the end of the story discuss together how the story is obviously African. What was Nomsa's house like? What animals appear in the story that are not found living wild in Britain? What was special about the Sangoma? What was different about him? What was the climate like? How did the people dress? What were the customs regarding gender that were in the story? How was the people's celebration of their customs different from our own? How was their celebration the same as ours? What are mielie and putu? (There is a glossary at the end of the story, for the less familiar terms.) Do we use mielie for anything? (cornflakes, corn on the cob and sweetcorn)

- Read 'The Chilli Challenge' and 'A Strange Meeting'. Again, discuss together the aspects of each culture that are shown in each story's narrative. Make available reference books and other sources of information to enable the children to explore the cultures in more depth in their group activities.

- If there are children in the class from the featured cultures, encourage them to share some experiences with the other children. Ask parents or other adults to come into school and bring items to show that are typical of the culture. Write letters to the embassies of the countries, asking for literature and information about the culture and lifestyle.

With the lower-achievers

With adult support

Choose from:

1   Revisit 'Nomsa and the Baboons' and together discuss how Nomsa's way of life is different from that in Britain. Explore the housing, food, clothes, customs, animals and climate. Help the children to find what parts of the story tell us

these things. Look again at 'The Chilli Challenge' and 'A Strange Meeting' and help them to compare elements of the British lifestyle with that in each story. Make a class book with writings and illustrations to show the culture of each of the countries featured in *The Chilli Challenge and other stories.*

2 Using Resource sheet 11a, help the children to complete the sentences about Nomsa's lifestyle and their own. Give support where necessary. They should then make the spinners and spin them to find an area of research. Help them to use reference books to find the information.

3 Make a book, written and illustrated by the children, of the culture of the country in which they live and go to school. Have a double-page spread on each of the following topics: homes, animals, clothes and weather. Put it on display with books on other cultures.

Teacher-independent activities

Choose from:

1 Let the children work as a group and choose one of the stories featured in *A Chilli Challenge and other stories.* Ask them to make a play about the story and practise acting it. Encourage them to write a play script to work from. Remind them to include the cultural elements that they explored during the whole-class session.

2 Let the children complete Resource sheet 11a. They could work in pairs to do the second section.

3 Ask the children to work in pairs and choose to be Sonny, Nomsa or Jack. They should write the story in the 1st person, making sure they mention the cultural elements that were discussed during the whole-class session.

Plenary session

■ Discuss the differences between the different cultures the children have been hearing about. Compare those cultures with your own. Which type of weather would the children prefer? Which type of home would they rather live in? Would they like to live near lions and baboons?

Lesson Two

Intended learning

■ To understand and use correctly the term 'preposition'.

■ To identify prepositions.

With the whole class

■ Write on the board some prepositions such as 'across', 'through', 'beside' and 'under'. Ask for volunteers to tell you what they are. If they don't use the term 'preposition', can they give you an explanation of what the words are? Does anybody know what they are called?

■ Write 'preposition' on the board and read it with the children. Explain that this is the term we use for words that tell us something about the position between two words, usually nouns, for example 'The cup was on the table.' Ask the children to give you sentences using the prepositions on the board. Invite volunteers to come and write more examples of prepositions alongside yours. Tell them you will leave the list on the board and they may add new ones to it whenever they find some.

■ Read through *The Chilli Challenge and other stories* again and look for prepositions. For example, the baboons in the mielie crop, Jack's visit to the Murray River or the children at Sonny's grandma's.

■ Play 'Quick-fire Prepositions'. Set a target time (you could use an egg-timer) and see how many prepositions the children can identify in sentences you say to them within that time. Challenge them to achieve the same number in less time.

With the lower-achievers

With adult support

Choose from:

1 Make sure the children know what prepositions are and that they can identify them. Check that they can use the term correctly. Copy and mount onto card Generic sheets 9 (page 126)

and 11 (page 128). Cut out the cards and mix them up together. Place them in a 'feely' bag. The children take turns to take out a card and say whether or not it is a preposition.

2   Give the children copies of Resource sheet 11b and help them to supply the appropriate prepositions for the sentences and pictures.

3   Help the children to write captions for the classroom displays, using appropriate prepositions.

4   Write some prepositions on a copy of Generic sheet 2 (page 119) and ask the children to follow the stages to learn how to spell the words. One of the words they have to learn could be 'preposition'.

Teacher-independent activities
Choose from:

1   Let the children complete Resource sheet 11b in pairs for reading support.

2   Make some preposition cards using Generic sheet 9 (page 126). Let the children play 'Preposition Charades'. The cards are placed face down on the table. The children should take a card, read it and mime the preposition.

3   Ask the children to draw a picture which shows as many prepositions as possible. For example, there could be transport going under and over bridges, through tunnels and so on. They should label the picture with the prepositions.

Plenary session

■   Play a game of 'Preposition Charades' using the preposition cards. Are the children able to identify all the prepositions mimed?

■   Did anybody find new or different prepositions? Look at the list drawn up during the whole-class session. Has it been added to?

■   Is everybody confident about using the term 'preposition'? Do they all understand what it means? Check that all the children can identify the common prepositions.

Lesson Three

Intended learning

■   To understand how a word can be transformed to mean its opposite by the addition of a prefix.

■   To understand negation with the prefix 'un' and to explore other prefixes that negate words.

With the whole class

■   Write on the board 'comfortable', 'happy', 'selfish', 'fold' and 'equal'. Ask the children to read them and tell you what they mean. Ask them what the opposite words are (uncomfortable, unhappy, unselfish, unfold and unequal). Let some of them write the words on the board beside each positive one. Ask a volunteer to say what happens to each of the words to change its meaning. Let them come out and use a different colour to highlight the prefix 'un' by circling it.

■   What does the term 'prefix' mean? If the children can't remember, take a few moments to remind them. Explain that adding the prefix 'un' before the word makes the negative or reverses it. Does everybody know what negative means? If not, explain it to them by reading a definition from a dictionary.

■   Ask the children to tell you some more negative words that start with 'un', such as 'unpopular', 'unfasten' and 'unsafe'. List them on the board and then ask the children what the opposite of each word is. Let them come and write them on the board.

■   Encourage the children to tell you some other prefixes that negate a word, for example, 'dis', 'im' or 'il'. Invite them to give you examples of words that have these prefixes. Write these on the board and tell them they may add any new words they find to the list while working in their groups. Leave the three lists up while working on this lesson.

■   Select some examples from the stories in *The Chilli Challenge and other stories* and add these to the list on the board.

With the lower-achievers

With adult support

Choose from:

1   Make sure the children understand what a prefix is. If necessary, spend more time exploring prefixes and how they affect words. Work together to find as many 'un' and 'dis' words as possible. Let them look at the lists written during the whole-class session for support. Help them to use a dictionary to find out what the words mean.

2   Give out copies of Resource sheet 11c. Help the children to read the words and put 'un' or 'dis' in front of them. They should then find more of each type in the dictionary. Help them to find some of the 'un' and 'dis' words in the grid.

3   Using Generic sheet 10 (page 127), help the children to make a word wheel. They should rotate the wheel until they can make sensible 'un' or 'dis' words. Ask them to use some of the words in sentences to show they have understood their meaning.

Teacher-independent activities

Choose from:

1   Let the children complete Resource sheet 11c in pairs for support.

2   Ask the children to choose six (or more, according to level of achievement) negative words from the lists written during the whole-class session. They should find them in the dictionary and write what they mean. Challenge them to find the opposite (positive) meanings and definitions.

3   Let the children work in pairs to make word wheels using Generic sheet 10 (page 127). They should rotate the wheels to make as many 'un' and 'dis' words as they can.

Plenary session

■   Together, rewrite a well-known story replacing the words with the opposites of the words traditionally used in the story. For example, 'Cinderella was very happy. Her stepmother and stepsisters were very kind to her. She had to undo all the cleaning in the house,' and so on.

■ Complete these sentences about the way you live and the way Nomsa lives. Use the words below to help you.

Nomsa's house is made from _____

My house is made from _____

For breakfast I eat _____ but

Nomsa eats _____

I usually see animals such as _____ There were

_____ in Nomsa's village.

The weather is usually _____ where Nomsa lives.

Where I live, it is usually _____

mud   mielie   baboons   cats   cool   bricks

straw   warm   rainy   dogs   cornflakes

■ Cut out these two spinners and make them as shown. Spin the spinners and wherever they stop these are your areas for research. Use books to find information about them.

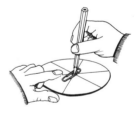

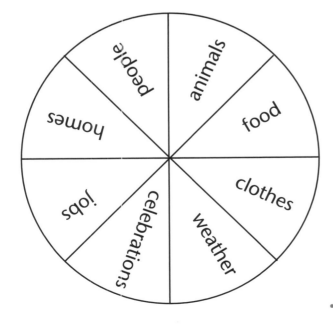

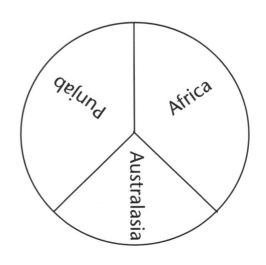

■ Choose a preposition to complete these sentences.

The thief ran _____ the road.

Six is the number _____ five and seven.

Our dog hid its bone _____ Dad's chair.

The lift went _____ to the top floor.

The train rattled _____ the tunnel.

Mum sat _____ me on the sofa.

behind	up	across	over	under	down	before
around		through		beside		between

■ Which prepositions go with these pictures?

_____   _____

■ Write a sentence for each of the three prepositions that are left.

_____

_____

_____

■ Find more prepositions and list them on the back of the sheet.

■ Write 'un' or 'dis' to make these words mean the opposite.

___happy   ___agree   ___safe   ___like

___selfish   ___true   ___allow   ___comfortable

___appear   ___like   ___honest   ___own

■ Find some more 'un' or 'dis' words in the dictionary.

_____   _____

_____   _____

■ In the grid below are hiding some of the words from the top of the page. Circle the words you find. You will find some others too.

u	n	s	a	f	e	e	t	t
n	u	u	n	d	u	k	s	e
h	s	n	i	d	n	i	e	r
a	i	d	d	i	d	l	n	u
p	d	o	i	s	i	s	o	s
p	l	s	i	d	s	i	h	n
y	n	w	o	s	i	d	s	u
n	e	u	r	t	n	u	i	s
e	e	r	g	a	s	i	d	u

unhappy ↓

disagree ←

unsafe →

dislike ↑

untrue ←

disown ←

undo ↓

dishonest ↑

unsure ↑

Stories from a point of view

Overall aims

- To explore a text written from an unusual viewpoint.
- To revise and use correctly the apostrophe for possession.
- To explore transforming words to form comparatives.

Featured book

War Horse by Michael Morpurgo, Collins Educational, 1999

Book synopsis

The story is told by Joey, a young horse from a farm in Devon. He finds himself taken from Albert, his beloved young master, and sold to the army for active service in France during the Great War. He tells of his experiences in battle, as an equine prisoner of war and his duties both in front of and behind the line of action. His horrendous adventure in no-man's-land ends with his admission to the veterinary hospital where he is delighted to be reunited with Albert. After a tense episode where he is threatened with the slaughterhouse, Joey finally returns to his home on the Devon farm, to end his days in peace.

Lesson One

Intended learning

- To explore a text written from an unusual viewpoint.
- To discuss how this affects the story and the reader's response.

With the whole class

Work on the first chapter will take one session. To complete the book may take several sessions.

- Show the cover of the book to the children and discuss together what the story might be about. Tell them that the book is written in the first person and is set during the First World War. Ask for ideas about who the narrator might be. List their suggestions and then read the author's note and Chapter 1.

- When you have read Chapter 1 together, explore some of the following ideas. Did anybody predict that the horse would be the narrator? Why is this so unusual? Would the story be different if told by Albert? Why or why not? Is the reader more sympathetic to Joey as the narrator? Why or why not? Ask the children to suggest how the story would alter if Albert was telling it. Encourage them to give reasons for their answers. Is the story more realistic for being told by Joey? Why or why not? Is the reader able to understand better Joey's feelings? Why or why not? Do the children think that the opening description of Joey's life in Devon will make a good contrast with later descriptions of the war? Encourage them to explain why or why not.

- Do the children know other stories that are told from the point of view of an animal (for example, 'I, Houdini' or 'Black Beauty')? Put together a collection of these stories and make them available for the children to read.

- Tell the children that they are going to do some activities before reading the rest of the book.

With the lower-achievers

With adult support

Choose from:

1 Explore some passages from Chapter 1 that help to convey the horse's point of view, for example the grooming on page 11 or the description of cruelty on page 9. Challenge the children to say how these passages are more realistic when told by the horse. How does empathising with the horse make the children feel when reading the descriptions? Encourage them to think of other unusual narrators, for example a car, a dog or an old armchair. Let them choose an unusual narrator and help them to write a short piece.

2 Together discuss how Zoey would have felt at the hands of Albert's dad. What was she trying

to tell Joey as he watched the cruelty and again as Joey himself was beaten? Help the children to write a short dialogue between Zoey and Joey.

3   Using Resource sheet 12a, help the children to answer the questions about *War Horse*. They should then write a short piece, told from Albert's point of view in the first person, about how he felt when Joey was brought home.

Teacher-independent activities

Choose from:

1   Let the children work in pairs to decide how the episode of cruelty in Chapter 1 would be described by Zoey (instead of Joey). They should write their description or record it on a cassette.

2   Give the children copies of Resource sheet 12a to complete in pairs for support. Read it through with them first before letting them work independently.

3   Ask the children to choose one episode from Chapter 1 of *War Horse* and practise retelling it in their own words, in the first person, as if Joey was speaking. Tell them that each child should tell part of the story before handing on to the next child.

Plenary session

■   Together write a short story from an unusual point of view. You could make it an emotive subject, such as the fox's story of a group of people on a day out foxhunting, or an amusing story, such as from the point of view of the wolf in Little Red Riding Hood.

Working with the whole book

■   Read the rest of *War Horse*. Discuss with the children some of the following points. Is the story more realistic for being told by Joey? Why or why not? Is the reader able to understand better Joey's feelings? Why or why not? How would the story be different if told by the other people who owned Joey? Encourage the children to explore how the story would have

been if, for example, it was told by Albert. Does Joey's narrative give a greater insight into the terror of war? Why or why not? Is there a moral or message behind the story? Ask the children to say what it is (for example, the futility of war, kindness to animals and so on).

Lesson Two

Intended learning

■   To revise and use correctly the apostrophe for possession.

■   To use the text as a basis for identifying examples.

With the whole class

■   Write on the board 'the dog's tail'. Remind the children of the work they did in Year 4 about apostrophes for possession. Point to the apostrophe in the sentence you have written and ask someone to tell you what it is called. Ask someone else to tell you what the phrase on the board says and what the apostrophe is for. Ask for more examples using the apostrophe in the singular, such as 'David's football' or 'Waseem's book'. Let the children write them on the board, using a different colour for the apostrophe 's' of each example.

■   Now ask for some examples of the use of an apostrophe in the plural, such as 'the dogs' tails', 'the players' football boots' or 'the cars' wheels'. Write them on the board. Invite a volunteer to tell you what the difference is between the two sets of examples.

■   Write on the board some irregular plurals such as 'children', 'men' and 'women'. Explain to the children that these are irregular plurals – for most nouns we add an 's' to the end of a word for the plural but there are some words that don't fit that rule so they are called 'irregular'. Ask the children if they can think of other examples of irregular plurals (people, deer, sheep). Explain that with these words the possessive apostrophe is in a different place than with other plurals. By 'the dog's tail' and 'the dogs' tails' written on the board, write 'the men's shoes'. This time the phrase is in the plural but after 'men' comes 's instead of s'. Do some more of these to make sure the children understand.

■ Show the children some examples of the possessive apostrophe in *War Horse*. 'Albert's mother' (page 23), 'Topthorn's nose' (page 88), 'No Man's Land' (page 97), 'Joey's picture' (page 110) and 'Emilie's horse' (page 134). (There are no examples of plural apostrophes in the text.)

With the lower-achievers

With adult support

Choose from:

1   Make sure that the children fully understand the use of the apostrophe, particularly for plurals. (Irregular plurals may well need some extra practice with lower-achievers.) Work with some more examples: 'the dogs' bones', 'the boxes' lids', 'the girls' shoes', 'the horses' hooves', 'the children's coats', 'the people's chairs' or 'the men's jackets'. Let the children practise writing on the board so that errors can be easily corrected.

2   Give out copies of Resource sheet 12b and help the children to join the pictures of the owners to their possessions. They should then complete the sentences with the correct use of the apostrophe. Help them to write sentences on the back of the sheet using the rest of the owner words.

3   Prepare a set of cards with pictures of owners, either singular or plural. (You could use magazines or comics for the pictures and stick them onto card.) Provide each child with two cards with 's and ' written on them. Play 'Apostrophe Flash' where you hold up a picture and the children have to hold up the correct apostrophe card as quickly as they can. Let them take turns to tell you something belonging to the owner on the card. They can be as silly as they like, for example 'dogs' umbrellas'.

Teacher-independent activities

Choose from:

1   Let the children complete Resource sheet 12b in pairs for support.

2   Prepare two sets of cards, one set with a singular or plural noun written on each and one set with 's or ' on each card. (Try to make the nouns as unconnected as possible, such as 'sausages', 'cars', 'monkey' or 'nappy'.) Let the children play a game where the noun cards are placed face down on the table, and the apostrophe cards in their respective piles are face up. The children should take two noun cards and join them with the correct apostrophe card. Challenge them to make some funny examples such as 'a monkey's nappy'.

3   Before the lesson, make a set of cards with owners and possessions written on them, for example 'The boys' skateboards'. Make sure you include some irregular plurals. Ask the children to read the cards, draw what the cards say and then complete a sentence such as 'The boys' skateboards were broken.'

Plenary session

■ Did some of the children make up funny or silly possession examples? Let them share these with everybody. Invite the children to make them even sillier. Ask them to tell you the correct use of the apostrophe for the owner(s).

■ Does everybody understand how the apostrophe is used for singular, plural and irregular plural possessives? Let some of the children write an owner on the board and others give them the correct use of the apostrophe. Do they remember both types of plural?

Lesson Three

Intended learning

- To explore transforming words to form comparatives.

- To understand and use comparatives.

With the whole class

- Ask the children to give you some examples of adjectives and let them write them on the board, for example 'big', 'green', 'high' and 'loud'. Point to 'loud' and ask *"How would we describe something that was more loud?"* When everyone is agreed on 'louder', write 'er' beside the base word. Explore the other adjectives in the same way. Agree that to make these words 'more' we add 'er' to the base adjective.

- Point to 'loud' again. Discuss how we describe something that was the 'most' loud. When they are agreed that we add 'est' (loudest) write this beside 'loud'. Do the same for all the adjectives. Agree that we add 'est' to the base adjective for the 'most'; not for 'more' which is 'er'.

- Write some 'base' words that end in 'y', such as 'pretty', 'funny' and 'dirty'. Ask the children how we change these words to show 'more' and 'most'. Explain that the 'y' changes to 'i', for example 'prettier' and 'prettiest', 'funnier' and 'funniest' and 'dirtier' and 'dirtiest'. Does anybody know other examples?

- Explain that we call these transformed words 'comparatives' because we are comparing different degrees of the same adjective. So 'quieter' is more than 'quiet' but not as much as 'quietest'. Say that other ways of making comparatives are by using 'more' and 'most'. Point out that when we use 'more' and 'most', we don't add 'er' and 'est' as well!

With the lower-achievers

With adult support

Choose from:

1   Make sure the children understand how we use comparatives. If necessary, give some more practice at transforming adjectives. Make cards using Generic sheet 11 (page 128). Hold up one card at a time and, as you show it, the children should tell you the comparative and the superlative adjectives. Give them a token for each correct answer. The winner is the child who has the highest number of tokens at the end of the game.

2   Using Resource sheet 12c, help the children to complete the table of comparatives. They should then complete the crossword.

3   Make a labelled chart showing some comparatives. The children could cut pictures from magazines and put them side by side to show, for example, a small flower, a smaller flower and the smallest flower or a tall person, a taller person and the tallest person.

Teacher-independent activities

Choose from:

1   Let the children work in pairs to complete Resource sheet 12c.

2   Give the children copies of Generic sheet 11 (page 128). They should write in each box the comparatives for each adjective. Challenge them to write sentences for some of the adjectives on the back of the sheet.

Plenary session

- Write some different adjectives on the board, such as 'pretty', 'lonely', 'wild', 'happy' and 'green'. Let individual children come to the board to write the comparatives for each. Point out that colours are also adjectives and have comparatives, as shown with 'green'.

- Tell the children that they cannot add 'er' or 'est' to every adjective. Sometimes they must use the words 'more' and 'most', for example with 'beautiful' and 'honest'.

■ Use the words in the box below to help you answer these questions about *War Horse.*

Who is the narrator? _____

Why is the narrator unusual? _____

Do you like this way of telling the story?_____

Why or why not? _____

_____

How did Joey feel the first time he had a halter put on?

_____

_____

| bewildered | Joey | frightened | dragged |
| kicking | experience | struggling | exhausted |

· ·

■ Pretend you are Albert. Write how you felt when Joey was brought home.

_____

_____

_____

_____

_____

_____

Continue on the back of this sheet.

■ Join the owners to their belongings ND then put ′ or ′s
at the end of each word.

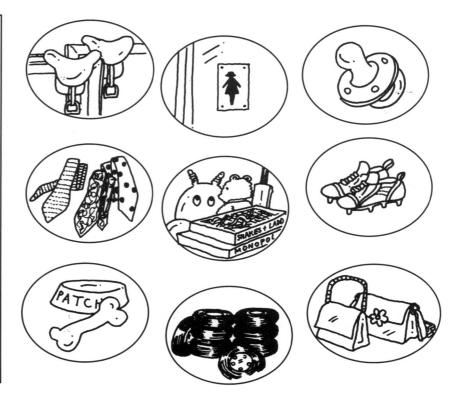

| ladies |
| boy |
| cars |
| dog |
| men |
| baby |
| horses |
| children |
| women |

■ Finish these sentences using some of the words above.

The _____ wheels fell off in the crash.

A robber ran into the _____ clothes shop.

Two cats took the _____ bone.

The _____ hooves thundered as they galloped across
the field.

■ Write two more sentences using some apostrophes.

_____

_____

■ Complete the table of comparatives.

	-er	-est
tiny	tinier	
big		biggest
pretty	prettier	
high	higher	
	louder	loudest
light		
funny		funniest
small		
quiet		
dirty		
	greener	

■ Complete this crossword.

ACROSS

1 Less than heavier.

4 More green.

5 Less than prettier.

7 Makes you laugh the most.

DOWN

2 Less than dirtier.

3 The most loud of all.

6 Less than tinier.

■ Write the comparatives of 'heavy', 'sunny' and 'black' on the back of the sheet.

Older stories

Overall aims

- To explore the appeal of older literature.
- To construct longer sentences using conjunctions.
- To use dictionaries efficiently.

Featured book

The Lion, the Witch and the Wardrobe by C S Lewis, (no specific edition recommended)

Book synopsis

The story is about four children – Lucy, Edmund, Susan and Peter – who are evacuated during the war to a large country house full of unused rooms that the children are eager to explore. Lucy, the youngest, goes through the back of a wardrobe into the magic land of Narnia, which is condemned to eternal winter by the White Witch. Lucy brings the other children into Narnia to meet the mythical creatures there. With the help of Aslan, a mystical lion, the children overcome the evil of the White Witch and free Narnia from the evil curse.

Lesson One

Intended learning

- To explore the appeal of older stories through listening to the chosen text being read aloud.
- To discuss how the language used reflects the age of the text.
- To form and justify an opinion about the text and express it by writing discursively.

With the whole class

Work on the first chapter will take one session. To complete the whole book may take several sessions.

- Show *The Lion, the Witch and the Wardrobe* to the children and ask whether anybody knows the story. Has anybody seen a dramatised version of it? Did they enjoy it? Read the first chapter of the book and encourage the children to express opinions about the opening of the story. Do

they want to know what happens next? Why or why not? Ask the children whether they can tell from the language if the story was written a long time ago or recently. Encourage them to explain their answers, for example would we hear modern children speaking in this way?

- Look at the conversation between the children on the opening pages. How is this different from the way we speak to each other today? For example, would we say 'Perfectly splendid', 'Come off it!', 'Trying to talk like Mother' or 'There's sure to be a row if we're heard talking here'? Ask the children to paraphrase some of the speeches using modern terms. Does this 'old-fashioned' language lessen or add to the enjoyment of the story?

- Explain that they are going to do some group activities before reading the rest of the book.

With the lower-achievers

With adult support

Choose from:

1 Discuss some examples from Chapter 1 that show the book was not written recently. For example, the Professor has a housekeeper and three servants, the children mentioned the wireless and the wardrobe is full of fur coats. Invite somebody to suggest why a story written today would probably not have fur coats in it. Explore again the way that the children in the book speak to each other and decide which parts of their conversations would not be heard today. Help them to record some of their suggestions and tell them you will look at these again after the book has been finished.

2 Give the children copies of Resource sheet 13a and help them to decide what they would say today in place of the words and phrases from the book. They should then complete the sentences about which of the children they would like as a friend and about the opening of the story.

3 Read one or two other older stories together, such as 'Peter Pan', 'A Little Princess' or 'The Borrowers'. Explore these in terms of the language, the story content, the characterisation and so on. Help the children to form opinions

and express them. Make a 'Book reviews' class book with reviews and opinions about the stories explored together written by the children. Leave it in the class library for the others to read.

Teacher-independent activities

Choose from:

1   Ask the children to complete Resource sheet 13a in pairs for support.

2   Give the children copies of Generic sheet 5 (page 122). They should make notes about the story, its characters and its setting. On the back they could draw a labelled picture of one or more of the children to show what they think they looked like.

3   Challenge the children to practise a role-play of the opening chapter. Remind them to use the 'old-fashioned' language in their dialogues. Let them refer to the book.

Plenary session

■ Read the second chapter of *The Lion, the Witch and the Wardrobe*. Is this what the children expected would happen? What other clues are there that the book was written a long time ago? What do they think of the development of the characters? Are they enjoying the story?

Working with the whole book

■ Tell the children you are going to read the rest of the book over the next couple of weeks or so. They should try to decide what it is about the book that helps it to retain its appeal. Encourage them to form an opinion about the story.

■ After reading the book, discuss together some of these points. Did the children enjoy the book? Why or why not? Did they enjoy it all the way through or were there parts which were less interesting? Encourage them to say why. Was it more interesting as the story progressed? Was the story itself appealing or exciting or frightening (or a mixture of all of these)? Why or why not? Were the children in the book realistic? Were they likeable? How did the language used to describe the children help us to form an opinion of them?

■ Discuss the descriptions of some of the characters, for example the Faun in Chapter 1, the White Witch in Chapter 3 or Aslan in Chapter 12. How does the language help the children visualise these characters? Do the descriptions help them to imagine how the characters behave or feel or think?

■ Discuss the story together, encouraging the children to form an opinion about it. Ask *"Was the story exciting? Do you think Aslan was foolish to sacrifice himself? Did his sacrifice help to conquer the evil? What do you think of each of the children? Why do you think this?"* Help the children to write a review of the book, expressing their opinion and justifying it.

■ Invite the children to suggest why the book is still popular so many years after it was written, for example the story is exciting, the children are realistic, the theme of good conquering evil is timeless and so on.

Lesson Two

Intended learning

■ To use the chosen text to examine conjunctions.

■ To construct longer sentences using conjunctions.

With the whole class

■ Before the session, write on the board a few pairs of sentences such as 'Mum went shopping' and 'There wasn't much food in the house', or 'The football team won 3–0' and 'There were only nine players'. Challenge the children to join each pair of sentences with a word, to make one longer sentence. For example, 'Mum went shopping because there wasn't much food in the house' or 'The football team won 3–0 although there were only nine players.' Let the children come and write the joining words on the board in a different colour. Ask if anybody knows what these words are called.

- Write 'conjunctions' on the board and read it with the children. Explain that reading can become boring if a passage is composed of short sentences. Two or more sentences can be joined together with a conjunction to make more interesting reading. Write on the board 'but', 'because', 'although' and 'so'. Tell the children that these are also conjunctions. Ask them to think of more examples. Let them come and add them to your list.

- Together agree some sentences that use each of the conjunctions in the list. You could start them off with an example such as 'England lost the World Cup but won the European Grand Prix.' Write the agreed sentences on the board. Leave them up while working on this lesson.

- Read some passages from *The Lion, the Witch and the Wardrobe*, telling the children to listen for conjunctions. Where there are conjunctions, read the sentence again as separate parts. Do they make sense? Are they as interesting? Are they as descriptive?

With the lower-achievers

With adult support

Choose from:

1 Write six different conjunctions on slips of paper and stick each one to a side of a cube to make a 'conjunctions dice'. Play a game where the children have to roll the dice and then say a sentence using the conjunction on the upper face when the dice has landed. Give writing support where necessary.

2 Give out copies of Resource sheet 13b. Help the children to join the sentences using the conjunctions and then complete some other sentences. They should then find the conjunctions in the grid at the bottom of the sheet. Give support where necessary.

3 Make cards with a conjunction written on each one and pin them at various points around the walls in the hall or gym. Call out sentences which include a conjunction (trying not to emphasise it, to make the children listen carefully). The children have to run to the appropriate conjunction card. You could play the game by calling individual children if you

wanted to avoid copying, but make the game fun and without pressure.

Teacher-independent activities
Choose from:

1 Give the children copies of Resource sheet 13b to complete. They could work in pairs for support.

2 Give the children copies of Generic sheet 2 (page 119) with conjunctions written on it. Ask them to work in pairs to learn the spellings using the 'Look, Say, Cover, Write, Check' strategy.

3 Make a 'conjunctions dice' as described in the adult-led activity. Let the children play a game where they have to roll the dice and then say a sentence using the conjunction on the upper face of the dice.

Plenary session

- Play a conjunction game using the 'conjunction dice' you made. Let one child come to the front, roll the dice and read out the word that is uppermost. The others have to think of a sentence using the word and put up their hands. The child who rolled the dice chooses one of them and asks them to say their sentence. If that person's sentence is correct, they come and roll the dice.

Lesson Three

Intended learning

■ To use dictionaries efficiently by using alphabetical order.

■ To revise, understand and use correctly the term 'alphabetical order'.

With the whole class

Before the session, write on the board several words from the Medium Frequency Word List in the *NLS*, but out of alphabetical order. Also have some dictionaries ready.

■ Does everybody remember what 'alphabetical order' means? Ask a volunteer to explain. If necessary, remind them. Read together the words on the board. Invite a volunteer to come and put the words into alphabetical order.

■ Write some of the children's names, including surnames, on the board. Agree the correct alphabetical order. Discuss what to do when two surnames begin with the same letter. What if the first two or three letters are the same, such as Waters and Watson? Do the same where the first four letters are the same – Wates and Waterford.

■ Ask the children how we would order two identical family names; by ordering the first names, for example Smith (John) and Smith (Michael). If there are no duplicate family names in the class, show the children some examples in a telephone directory.

■ Talk about the characters in *The Lion, the Witch and the Wardrobe*. Write their names on the board in alphabetical order with the children telling you which to write next.

With the lower-achievers

With adult support

Choose from:

1   Using Resource sheet 13c, help the children to place the words in alphabetical order.

2   Give out copies of Generic sheets 9 (page 126) and 11 (page 128). Ask the children to cut out the words and paste them in alphabetical order onto a large sheet of paper. Help them to look in a dictionary for the first and last words in the list and write their definitions.

Teacher-independent activities

Choose from:

1   Make cards with the words on Generic sheets 9 (page 126) and 11 (page 128). The children have to put them into alphabetical order on a table or the floor. Tell them to time themselves the first time, then shuffle the cards and do it again seeing if they can beat their first time.

2   Ask the children to complete Resource sheet 13c in pairs. Read it through with them before letting them work independently.

3   Challenge the children to write the names of everyone in the class (or group, depending on level of achievement) in alphabetical order.

Plenary session

■ Write on the board a random selection of ten words from *The Lion, the Witch and the Wardrobe*. Ask for volunteers to look for them in the dictionary. How long does it take to check all the words? Can the children beat their own record?

■ Play an alphabetical game, such as 'I went to market and I bought an apple…'

■ Read these words and phrases from Chapter 1 of
The Lion, the Witch and the Wardrobe. Then write
beneath each one what you would say instead.

wireless   perfectly splendid

_____   _____

Come off it!   simply enormous

_____   _____

Peter   Edmund   Lucy   Susan

■ Which of the children would you like as a friend?

_____

■ Why? _____

_____

■ Complete this sentence.

I liked/did not like the opening of the story because

_____

_____

■ Join these pairs of sentences with a conjunction from the list.

and   **but**   **because**   **so**   **although**

Mum went shopping _____ we had no food.

The team won 3–0 _____ we only had 9 players.

Jo did the washing _____ then she did the ironing.

I want to buy a car _____ I don't have enough money.

Dad was hungry _____ he ate a whole cake.

■ Complete these sentences.

The baby was crying because _____

The boy went to bed although _____

We went to school and _____

■ Find the conjunctions in the grid.

a	n	d	e	w	b	e	e
l	e	x	c	h	e	x	x
t	o	e	n	e	c	c	c
h	w	e	i	n	a	e	e
o	h	f	i	t	u	b	p
u	m	i	g	o	s	d	t
g	e	x	w	h	e	x	c
h	x	s	i	n	c	e	f

and
although
but
because
so
except
if
since
when

Name _____

■ Write these words in alphabetical order.

number	dentist	round	history
weight	address	freeze	monster

1. _____   2. _____

3. _____   4. _____

5. _____   6. _____

7. _____   8. _____

■ Now try these.

that	three	this	thread	think	thank

1. _____   2. _____   3. _____

4. _____   5. _____   6. _____

■ Write these children's names in the order they would appear in the class register.

Paul Waters   _____

Thomas Smith   _____

Mike Somers   _____

Iqbal Bassra   _____

Mandy Somerton   _____

Surinder Soni   _____

Jill Smith   _____

Susan Walters   _____

Poems from other cultures

Overall aims

- To read and explore poems from a different culture.
- To use the chosen poems as a stimulus for exploring the culture.
- To use the poetry as a basis for own work.

Featured book

A Caribbean Dozen, edited by John Agard and Grace Nichols, Walker Books, 1994

Lesson One

Chosen poem

'The Pow-Wow Drum' by David Campbell, page 105

Intended learning

- To read and explore the chosen poem.
- To use the poem as a stimulus for own poetry.
- To use the chosen poem as a stimulus for exploring the culture and history of Native Americans.

With the whole class

- Enlarge a copy of 'The Pow-Wow Drum'. Tell the children they are going to read a poem by David Campbell about Native Americans. What is a 'powwow'? (A meeting, conference.) Ask for volunteers to find 'powwow' in the dictionary. Ask the children what a powwow drum would be used for. Explain that it was an important part of the powwow.

- Read 'The Pow-Wow Drum', letting the children follow the text. Where do the people in this poem come from? How do we know? ('Leave the dusty cities far behind') When is the poem set? How do we know? ('The old and young meeting like they did long ago') Where have the tribes from long ago gone? Why do today's Native Americans gather in this way?

- Read the chorus again. What does it make the children think of? Does its rhythm make them imagine the beating of the drum?

- Explain to the children how the Europeans massacred the Native Americans for their lands, how their tribes were put onto reservations and deprived of any rights, how Christianity was introduced and how the culture of western Europe became the basis of American culture, at the expense of that of the Native Americans.

- Look at some of the phrases in the poem. What do the children think 'the feet of lightning' means? What are the 'long black braids'? Ask them why 'Fancy dancers free under the sky' is such an important phrase. Remind them that the Native Americans were put onto reservations and lost their freedom. What does 'we come again to dance again' imply? Explain that dance plays an important part in a powwow. What does 'Answering the beat of the pow-wow drum' mean?

- Together write another verse for the poem. On the board, list related items such as the feathered headdresses, the sacred pipe, holy relics such as sacred bones and so on. Draft some lines for the new verse and add 'we come again to dance again' and the chorus. Encourage the children to change and rewrite the lines until they are satisfied. Write the final version on the board.

- Tell the children they are going to explore Native American culture in their groups.

With the lower-achievers

With adult support

Choose from:

1 Read the poem again with the children, making sure they understand the ideas that were explored in the whole-class session. Using Resource sheet 14a, help them to decide what the phrases from 'The Pow-Wow Drum' mean. Give reading support if necessary.

2 This activity may need to be done away from the main classroom. Using drums, help the children to make up a ritual dance, chanting from the poem and using the rhythm of the chorus to set the beat. You could allocate

different lines to different children and let them all join in with ' we come again to dance again' and the chorus. If possible, let the children dress in costume.

3   Give out copies of Resource sheet 14b and help the children to look in the dictionary for the words on the sheet. They should write the meanings in their own words and then match the words to the illustrations. Help them to write a poem about the Native Americans.

4   Together, explore books about the colonisation of America. Help the children to discover how the opening of the American west meant the loss of the Native Americans' way of life. Write 'tepee', 'bison' and 'powwow' on the board. Help the children to find the words in reference books and to write about each topic.

Teacher-independent activities

Choose from:

1   Give the children copies of Resource sheet 14a to complete in pairs. Read it through with them before letting them work independently.

2   Ask the children to practise a role-play about the powwow. They should include as much of the poem as possible in their performance.

3   Let the children complete Resource sheet 14b, again in pairs for support.

Plenary session

■   Let the children who made up a ritual dance or who practised a role-play of the powwow give a class performance.

■   Encourage some of the children to share what they have learned about the Native American way of life. Let them show their writing and illustrations to the others.

Lesson Two

Chosen poem

Extract from 'Sioux Rite of the Sacred Pipe', (traditional), page 106

Intended learning

■   To read and discuss the chosen poem, expressing an opinion about it.

■   To use the chosen poem as a stimulus for exploring the culture of Native Americans.

■   To use the poem as a stimulus for own poetry.

With the whole class

■   Enlarge a copy of 'Sioux Rite of the Sacred Pipe'. Tell the children that this poem is from the culture of the Sioux. Do any of the children know who the Sioux are? Explain that they are a Native American tribe. Use a globe to find North America and track the route from there to Britain. Explain that the Sioux were conquered by white settlers and pioneers and put onto reservations after their land was confiscated.

■   Read the title together. Encourage the children to suggest what it might mean. Point to 'Pipe' and ask if anybody knows what kind of pipe it is. Explain that the sacred pipe was smoked by the leaders of the tribe. They would pass it around at important ceremonies such as tribe deliberations, peacemaking conferences and so on. Together look in dictionaries for a definition of 'rite'.

■   Read 'Sioux Rite of the Sacred Pipe' to the children, letting them follow the text. Ask them what it is about. Explain that it is a prayer to the Great Spirit, asking him to protect all people throughout their lives.

■   Focus on some of the phrases in the poem and explore together what they mean, for example who is 'my Grandfather'? (A deity much like the Christian God the Father or Muslim Allah.) Who are the 'children without number'? (Countless human beings.) Why is the wish that 'they may face the winds' a good thing? (In the world of nature, animals facing the wind can scent their predators early.) What does 'the day of quiet' mean? (Death, which is thought of in a positive way by the Sioux.)

■ Look at some of the other lines in the poem. For example, can the children tell you what 'All over the earth the faces of living things are alike' might mean? Explain that the Sioux thought all men were equal no matter what colour or race they were. Do the children think 'And walk the good road' is a good wish? Ask them to suggest what it means. Tell them that the wish is for people to live a happy life. Do they think this poem is different from or similar to 'The Pow-Wow Drum'? Why?

■ Invite the children to suggest other 'good wishes' for a further verse to the poem, for example that the crops may flourish, that their hunts may be successful, that they may have no tribal wars and so on. List their suggestions on the board and leave them there for reference during the group activities.

■ Agree one or two of the ideas and together write a few more lines for the main poem. Encourage the children to redraft and change anything with which they are not happy. Leave the final version on the board.

With the lower-achievers

With adult support

Choose from:

1 Read 'Sioux Rite of the Sacred Pipe' again with the children, encouraging them to join in where they can. Revisit some of the ideas explored during the whole-class session. Make sure they understand what the message of the poem is. Ask them to draw a picture of the Sioux chiefs gathered around smoking the pipe. Help them to write a short piece about their picture, explaining the importance of the ritual pipe.

2 Give out copies of Resource sheet 14c. Help the chilkdren to complete the sentences about the Sioux and then write a second part to the 'Sioux Rite of the Sacred Pipe'. Let them refer to the list of ideas and the new verse written during the whole-class session.

3 Working closely with the children, help them to find information about the culture of the Native Americans. Encourage them to find out about living conditions, food, clothes, rituals and how the tribes declined. Together, make a class book written and illustrated by the children. Give support where necessary.

Teacher-independent activities

Choose from:

1 Ask the children to practise a role-play of the rite, using some of the words or phrases from the 'Sioux Rite of the Sacred Pipe'. If practical, encourage them to use musical instruments to accompany their play.

2 Let the children complete Resource sheet 14c. They could work in pairs and refer to the list of ideas and the new verse written during the whole-class session.

3 Make available books about the Native Americans. Give each pair of children one area to investigate such as clothes, housing, food and so on. Let them write about their topic and illustrate their work. They could put their chapters together to make a class book.

Plenary session

■ Ask the children who practised a role-play to give a performance. Did they remember to include some words or phrases from the poem?

■ What have the children learned about the culture of Native Americans? Ask for volunteers to tell you about the different aspects they explored.

■ Read the 'Sioux Rite of the Sacred Pipe' once more, encouraging the children to join in.

The Pow-Wow Drum

Long black braids and silken
   shawls
Moving side by side where the
   eagle calls,
Answering the beat of the pow-
   wow drum
      we come again
      to dance again

Hey-a, Hey-a, Hey-a, Hey-a, Hey!
Hey-a, Hey-a, Hey-a, Hey-a, Hey!

Leave the dusty cities far
   behind,
Meet our brothers of the country
   with one mind,
Travelling from the east, north,
   south and west
      we come again
      to dance again

Hey-a, Hey-a, Hey-a, Hey-a, Hey!
Hey-a, Hey-a, Hey-a, Hey-a, Hey!

Watching close the feet of
   lightning fly
Fancy dancers free under the
   sky,
Joining in the circle moving
   round and round
      we come again
      to dance again

Hey-a, Hey-a, Hey-a, Hey-a, Hey!
Hey-a, Hey-a, Hey-a, Hey-a, Hey!

Women shining like the morning
   sun,
Children making rainbows as
   they laugh and run,
The old and young meeting like
   they did long ago
      we come again
      to dance again

Hey-a, Hey-a, Hey-a, Hey-a, Hey!
Hey-a, Hey-a, Hey-a, Hey-a, Hey!

David Campbell

Sioux Rite of the Sacred Pipe (extract)

Great Spirit, Great Spirit, my Grandfather,
All over the earth the faces of living things are alike;
With tenderness have these come up out of the ground;
Look upon these faces of children without number
And with children in their arms, that they may face the winds
And walk the good road to the day of quiet.

Traditional

■ Read these phrases from 'The Pow-Wow Drum'.

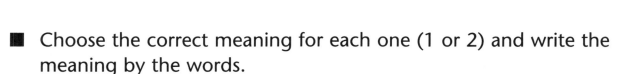

'Feet of lightning'

'Long black braids'

'Answering the beat of the pow-wow drum'

■ Choose the correct meaning for each one (1 or 2) and write the meaning by the words.

'Feet of lightning' = _____

1. A thunderstorm coming from the Native Americans' feet.

2. Very fast dancing.

'Long black braids' = _____

1. Long black hair in plaits.

2. Ropes that are black.

'Answering the beat of the pow-wow drum' = _____

_____

1. Sending a letter to the drummer.

2. Dancing to the rhythm of the drum.

■ Read these two lines from the poem.

Women shining like the morning sun,
Children making rainbows as they laugh and run

■ On the back of this sheet, illustrate these two lines from the poem. Talk with a friend about what the poet means.

■ Look in an adult's dictionary for these words and write the meanings in your own words.

   1. tepee   2. bison   3. powwow

1. _____

_____

_____

2. _____

_____

_____

3. _____

_____

■ Finish this poem about Native Americans. Use the words in the box below to help you.

The braves _____

And the chiefs _____

With feathers and paint they _____

_____

In battle and hunting _____

_____

> powwow buffalo   arrows   headdress
> warrior   sacred   bows   hunting

■ Look at this map and then complete the sentences.

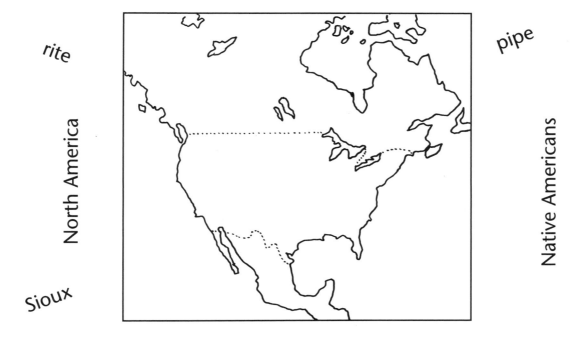

rite

pipe

North America

Native Americans

Sioux

This is a map of _____

It is where the _____ lived.

The Sioux was a tribe of _____

They believed that the _____was sacred.

■ Write a few more lines for the 'Sacred Pipe' poem. Use the words in the box below to help you.

Great Spirit, Great Spirit, my Grandfather

May the sun _____

All your people are _____

Let the moon _____

And the soft rain _____

| faithful | guide | fall | rise | peaceful |
| nourish | gently | warm | happy | shine | set |

Classic poems

Overall aims

- To read classic poems from recognised authors.

- To explore the language and the narrative, and how they relate to the poem's time.

- To discuss the poetry and express personal opinions about it.

- To use the chosen poems as a stimulus to explore other classic poetry.

Featured books

A First Poetry Book compiled by John Foster, Oxford University Press, 1979 (1989 edition)

Georgian Poets selected by James Reeves, Penguin, 1968

Lesson One

Chosen poem

'Windy Nights' by Robert Louis Stevenson, page 113

Intended learning

- To read and discuss the chosen poem, expressing a personal opinion about it.

- To explore the language of the poem and how it relates to its own time.

- To use the poem as a stimulus for own work.

With the whole class

- Tell the children they are going to read some poems by authors who lived long ago, but who are still popular today. Write 'Robert Louis Stevenson' on the board and ask the children whether they have heard of him. Tell them the correct pronunciation of Louis (silent 's').

- Enlarge a copy of 'Windy Nights'. Read the poem with the children, letting them follow the text. Ask them what they think the poem is about. Who is the man who gallops by in the night? Where is he going? Do they think there is a reason for the man going by only on very

stormy nights? Give them some starter suggestions, such as smuggling or stealing.

- Ask the children if they like the poem. Encourage them to give reasons for their answers. Are they frustrated because they never find out what the man's business is, or do they like the mystery? Do they find the atmosphere spooky, frightening or mysterious (or all three)? Encourage them to explain why they feel this.

- What clues are there that the poem was written a long time ago? Agree that the word 'gallop' implies he is riding a horse and that, while people still ride horses, they wouldn't ride all night so the horse was likely to be a mode of transport (before cars). Also, 'when the fires are out'; although there are still homes that have real fires they are becoming more and more a thing of the past.

- Encourage the children to identify words or phrases that are old-fashioned, for example 'highway' meaning 'road', 'goes he' and 'By at the gallop'. Explain that these are phrases not usually found in modern poetry.

- Do the children think the setting of the poem is the town or the country? What makes them think so?

- Together, write a third verse in the style of the poem. Brainstorm ideas that could throw some light on what the man's business is, and agree on one. Start the verse with:
'Whenever the rain is pouring down,
Whenever it's dark and drear,
The man on the horse once more will go...'

Encourage the children to change and redraft until everybody is satisfied with the verse. Leave it up while working on this lesson.

With the lower-achievers

With adult support

Choose from:

1   Make sure the children understand how we know that the poem was written long ago. Discuss again some of the points covered in the whole-class session. Help the children to learn the poem to recite during the plenary session. Encourage them to use intonation and actions to convey the atmosphere of the poem.

2   Give out copies of Resource sheet 15a. Help the children to decide which words or phrases are old-fashioned and which are modern. They should then choose some of the old-fashioned words and phrases from 'Windy Nights' that show it to be an old poem.

3   Challenge the children to rewrite the poem, substituting the old-fashioned words with modern-day ones.

4   Help the children to write the story of 'Windy Nights' in prose. Help them to use descriptive words that create an atmosphere and mystery like that of the poem.

Teacher-independent activities

Choose from:

1   Ask the children to complete Resource sheet 15a. They should work in pairs for this activity.

2   Organise the children to work in pairs to find information about Robert Louis Stevenson. (There is usually a short biography in *A Child's Garden of Verses*.) Ask them to make a book about him. You could give them a list of facts to find such as his birthplace, when he was born, what his job was, where he lived, when he died and so on.

3   Give the children one or two of Robert Louis Stevenson's other poems. Ask them to read these in pairs and discuss the words and phrases, using a dictionary to help them. They should choose some that are old-fashioned to share with the others during the plenary session.

Plenary session

■   Ask the children who learned the poem to give a class performance. Together, read the original once more including the verse jointly written during the whole-class session.

■   Ask the children who explored other poems by Robert Louis Stevenson to show the class the old-fashioned words and phrases they discovered. Were any of them difficult and do any need to be explained? Read the poems that the children chose.

Lesson Two

Chosen poem

'Echo' by Walter de la Mare, page 114

Intended learning

■   To read and discuss the chosen poem, expressing a personal opinion about it.

■   To explore the language of the poem and how it relates to its own time.

■   To use the chosen poem as a stimulus to explore other classic poetry.

With the whole class

■   Enlarge a copy of 'Echo'. Tell the children they are going to explore a poem by another classic poet, Walter de la Mare. Write the name on the board and ask the children whether they have heard of him.

■   Tell the children to close their eyes and then read the poem to them. Ask them what the poem is about. What is the atmosphere of the poem? Do they find it eerie, frightening or mysterious, or all three? Why do they think this? Who do they think owns the eyes and the voices in the poem?

■   Can they find an echo in the poem? Read again the lines together. Have the children ever experienced an echo of their voice? What was it like? Did it 'wail to and fro'?

■   Which words or phrases in the poem do the children think are old-fashioned? For example, 'Hither', 'thither', 'mockery', 'faintingly on' and so on. Are there any that they do not understand?

■   Using dictionaries, ask the children to find the meanings of 'glades', 'boughs' and 'brake'. Then ask them whether this poem is set in the town or the country. How do they know?

■   Read the poem one more time. As you read it the children could draw sketches of their impressions of the poem. Ask them to create the atmosphere of the poem.

With the lower-achievers

With adult support

Choose from:

1 Read the poem together once again, encouraging the children to join in. Make sure they understand all of the archaic expressions and words. Help them to recite the poem with expression.

2 Using Resource sheet 15b, help the children to find the old-fashioned words in the dictionary and match them to their meanings. Encourage them to write a short piece expressing their opinion of 'Echo'. Remind them they are allowed to say they don't like it.

3 Give the children copies of Resource sheet 15c and help them to complete the poem. Encourage them to write their own echo poem.

4 Look through other anthologies for poems by classic or long-established authors such as Alfred Noyes, Robert Louis Stevenson, Walter de la Mare, James Reeves or Ian Serraillier. Make a class anthology of the favourite poems, making sure each child's chosen poem is included.

Teacher-independent activities

Choose from:

1 Let the children complete Resource sheet 15b.

2 Let the children work in pairs to find some information about Walter de la Mare. Ask them to make a book about him. You could give them a list of facts to find such as his birthplace, when he was born, where he lived, when he died and so on.

3 Ask the children to complete Resource sheet 15c, working in pairs for support.

Plenary session

■ Let the children who explored other classic poems tell the class about their favourites. Read some of these to the children and let the group read others aloud.

■ Ask for volunteers to read their own echo poems to the rest of the class.

■ Read 'Echo' once again, encouraging the children to join in.

Windy Nights

Whenever the moon and the stars are set,
Whenever the wind is high,
All night long in the dark and wet,
A man goes riding by.
Late in the night when the fires are out,
Why does he gallop and gallop about?

Whenever the trees are crying aloud,
And ships are tossed at sea,
By, on the highway, low and loud,
By at the gallop goes he.
By at the gallop he goes, and then
By he comes back at the gallop again.

Robert Louis Stevenson

Echo

'Who called?' I said, and the words
Through the whispering glades,
Hither, thither, baffled the birds -
'Who called? Who called?'

The leafy boughs on high
Hissed in the sun;
The dark air carried my cry
Faintingly on:

Eyes in the green, in the shade,
In the motionless brake,
Voices that said what I said,
For mockery's sake:

'Who cares?' I bawled through my tears;
The wind fell low:
In the silence, 'Who cares? Who cares?'
Wailed to and fro.

Walter de la Mare

■ Read these words. Are they old or modern? Write 'old' or 'modern' beside each one.

disco _____ crib _____ jogging _____

maiden _____ byte _____ poesy

_____

■ Look in a dictionary for the words you don't know.

■ Read 'Windy Nights' and write some of the old-fashioned words or phrases.

_____   _____

_____   _____

■ Write another verse for 'Windy Nights' to tell what the man might be doing. You could choose your own words or use the words below.

Whenever the rain is pouring down
Whenever it's dark and drear,
The man on the horse once more will go

To _____

To _____ goes he

And _____

(comfort those in fear)   (visit his sweetheart dear)

(happy to see him is she)   (his coming they're
                                happy to see)

■ Look at these old words from the poem 'Echo' by Walter de la Mare.

glades   hither   boughs   brake   thither

■ Find the words in your teacher's dictionary and then match them with the meanings here.

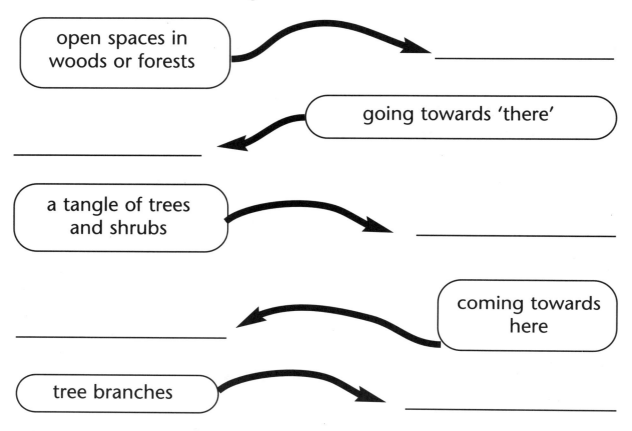

open spaces in woods or forests → _____

going towards 'there' ← _____

a tangle of trees and shrubs → _____

coming towards here ← _____

tree branches → _____

■ What did you think of 'Echo'? Use the words below to help you.

_____

_____

_____

mysterious   good   spooky   hard   scary   funny

boring   true   silly   interesting   old-fashioned

■ What does 'echo' mean? Look it up in a dictionary and write its meaning in your own words.

_____

■ What does 'mockery' mean? Look it up in a dictionary and write its meaning in your own words.

_____

■ Complete this poem. If you look carefully, you will find all the words you need.

The Echo

'Hello,' I shouted into the quiet air.

'_____' came back, from I
    know not where.

'Who's there?' I called. But no reply.

Except '_____?' I know not
    why.

'Come out,' I shouted, 'if you can.'

'_____' I heard from no
    woman or man.

'You're a coward!' I yelled. 'Too
    scared to come out!'

'_____!' was the echoing
    shout.

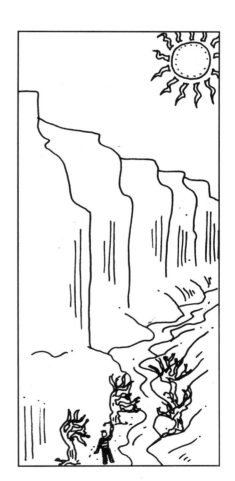

■ Write your own echo poem on the back of this sheet.

■ Follow the numbers.

5 Write

_____

1 Learn the
words under 2.

_____

_____

_____

_____

_____

2 Look

_____ _____

_____ _____

_____ _____

6 Check

_ _fold

3 Say

4 Cover

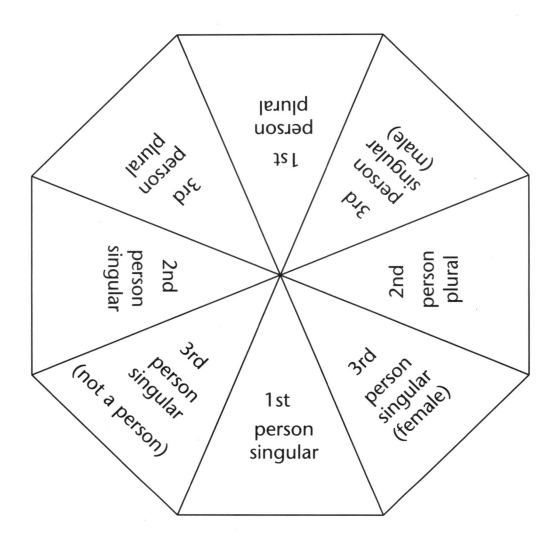

■ Make a spinning top by putting a cocktail stick through the centre.

I	you	he	she
it	we	you	they

Name _____

Story starters

Many years ago, before cars or aeroplanes or television, a young boy called Philip was living on a farm in the hills.

On my way to school last week something terrible happened to me – some aliens from a spaceship kidnapped me!

Although I'm now a princess, I was born a poor girl but thanks to the gentle dragon, my fortune changed and here's how it happened.

Uma was very excited because today was the start of Divali, one of the most important festivals in India.

Story planner

Title of story

....

Period of time story is set in

Setting where story takes place

Characters in the story

Story beginning

verb	past tense	present tense	future tense

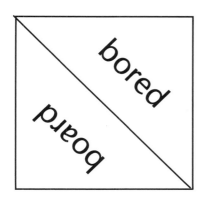

bored / board

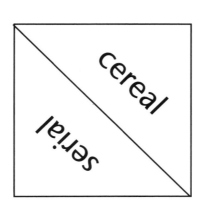

cereal / serial

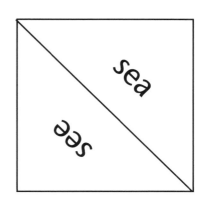

sea / see

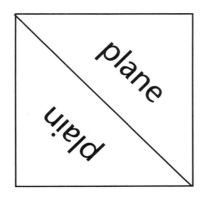

plane / plain

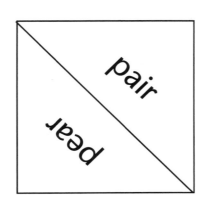

pair / pear

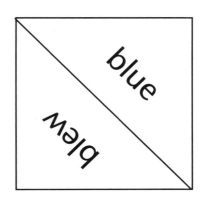

blue / blew

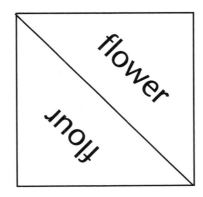

flower / flour

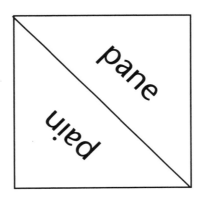

pane / pain

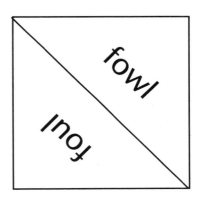

fowl / foul

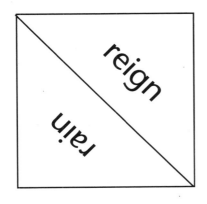

reign / rain

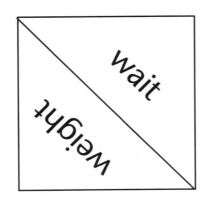

wait / weight

behind	around	up
through	across	beside
over	between	under
down	before	beneath

Name _____

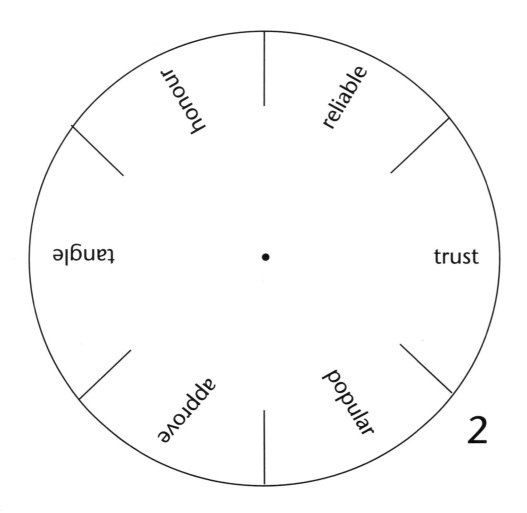

2

- Cut out both circles.

- Pin circle 1 to circle 2 with a split pin.

- Make words beginning with 'un' or 'dis'.

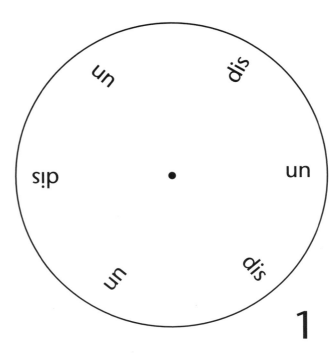

1

pretty	quiet	small
dirty	high	light
green	funny	loud
black	heavy	tiny